Map Reading, Latitude, Longitude & Time

BY
MYRL SHIREMAN

COPYRIGHT © 1998 Mark Twain Media, Inc.

ISBN 1–58037–079–9

Printing No. CD–1314

Mark Twain Media, Inc., Publishers
Distributed by Carson-Dellosa Publishing Company, Inc.

Table of Contents

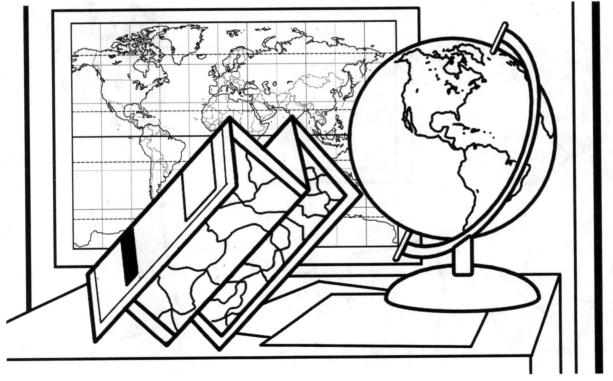

Introduction

Many students in secondary school and college have not developed map-reading skills and a basic understanding of longitude and latitude. Many students can verbalize the skills that relate to map reading, latitude, and longitude, but they cannot apply the skills in problem situations. Some of this is a result of the fact that most texts devote little time to the application of these skills. If students are to become proficient in map reading and the use of latitude and longitude, many opportunities for application must be provided.

The exercises in this book are designed for a wide range of students. The skills presented are designed to review and more fully develop skills introduced in the lower grades. The activities presented will reinforce and expand on the latitude and longitude skills presented in middle-grade texts.

The activities are designed so that the skills presented are reinforced through many map and diagram activities. The use of diagrams and maps ensures a better understanding of the skills relating to map reading, latitude, and longitude. Additionally, there is sufficient repetition of the skills to ensure understanding for students who are experiencing difficulties.

Maps located in a section at the back of the book will need to be copied for use with many of the activities.

The skills presented are developed from those that are the most basic to those that are more abstract. Some of the activities presented will challenge the most able students. However, the focus of this book is on developing and improving understanding for all middle-grade students.

Name_____ Date _____

Developing Map-Reading Skills

It is important to learn how to read maps. Maps are used to display all kinds of information. Maps may illustrate political, physical, climatic, religious, population, and other kinds of information.

Political maps show where the countries, capitals, and major cities are located. Physical maps show where features on the earth's surface, such as mountains, rivers, lakes, and plains, are located. Population maps show where people live. Using a population map, one can find where the major population centers are, as well as those areas where few people live.

Refer to the three maps below and answer the following questions.

Circle the correct answer and complete the statement for each.

1. Map A is a (political/physical/population) map because it shows

_____

_____

2. Map B is a (political/physical/population) map because it shows

_____

_____

3. Map C is a (political/physical/population) map because it shows

_____

_____

Name _____ Date _____

     To use a map, one must know how to read the map. On most maps, the top of the map is north. However, when using a map, it is important to check the **compass rose**. The compass rose is a symbol on the map that shows where north, south, east, and west are on the map. When a map does not contain a compass rose, assume that the top of the map is north, west is left, east is right, and south is at the bottom of the map.

Refer to the information just discussed and complete the blanks.

     Maps are made to show many different kinds of (1)_____.

Maps that show where rivers, lakes, mountains, and plains are located are known as

(2) _____ maps. Maps that show where people live are

(3)_____ maps. If one wants to know where a specific climate type is

located, it is necessary to use a (4)_____ map.

     When using a map, the (5)_____ _____ shows the directions

on the map. If no compass rose is shown, then the top of the map is (6) _____,

and the bottom of the map is (7)_____.

8. Color the compass rose below and label with **North**, **South**, **East**, and **West**.

Name _____ Date _____

The Map Legend

When using a map, an important tool is the **legend**. The legend shows the keys that are needed to read the map correctly. An important kind of information found in the legend is a **scale**. This scale tells how many miles a specific distance on the map represents on the earth.

Example: A map legend indicates that one inch on the map equals 100 miles on Earth. Then three inches on the map would equal 300 miles. 3 in. x 100 miles = 300 miles.

Answer the following questions.

The legend on a map indicates that each inch equals 50 miles. Show mathematical computation in the space to the right.

1. Two inches on the map equals _____ miles.

2. Five inches on the map equals _____ miles.

3. Ten inches on the map equals _____ miles.

The legend on a map indicates that each inch equals 100 miles. Show mathematical computation in the space to the right.

4. Two inches on the map equals _____ miles.

5. Five inches on the map equals _____ miles.

6. Ten inches on the map equals _____ miles.

The legend on a map indicates that each inch equals three miles. Show mathematical computation in the space to the right.

7. Two inches on the map equals _____ miles.

8. Five inches on the map equals _____ miles.

9. Ten inches on the map equals _____ miles.

Name _____ Date _____

Converting Kilometers to Miles

Increasingly, metric measurements are used on maps. A scale may indicate that one centimeter equals ten kilometers. You can convert the kilometer to miles. One kilometer equals 0.621 miles. To convert kilometers to miles, multiply times 0.621.
Example: 10 km x 0.621 = 6.21 miles. Ten kilometers equals 6.21 miles.

Determine how many kilometers are represented on the map. Then convert that answer to miles.

The legend on a map indicates that each centimeter equals 50 kilometers. Show mathematical computation in the space to the right. Round to the nearest mile.

1. Two cm on the map equals _____ kilometers. _____ miles.

2. Five cm on the map equals _____ kilometers. _____ miles.

3. Ten cm on the map equals _____ kilometers. _____ miles.

The legend on a map indicates that each centimeter equals 100 kilometers. Show mathematical computation in the space to the right. Round to the nearest mile.

4. Two cm on the map equals _____ kilometers. _____ miles.

5. Five cm on the map equals _____ kilometers. _____ miles.

6. Ten cm on the map equals _____ kilometers. _____ miles.

The legend on a map indicates that each centimeter equals three kilometers. Show mathematical computation in the space to the right. Round to the nearest tenth of a mile.

7. Two cm on the map equals _____ kilometers. _____ miles.

8. Five cm on the map equals _____ kilometers. _____ miles.

9. Ten cm on the map equals _____ kilometers. _____ miles.

Name _____ Date _____

Converting Miles to Kilometers

If you know the measurement in miles, you may want to convert it to kilometers. To convert miles to kilometers, multiply times 1.6.

Example: 10 miles x 1.6 = 16 km.

Determine how many miles are represented on the map. Then convert that answer to kilometers.

The legend on a map indicates that each inch equals 100 miles. Show mathematical computation in the space to the right.

1. Two inches on the map equals _____ miles. _____ kilometers.

2. Five inches on the map equals _____ miles. _____ kilometers.

3. Ten inches on the map equals _____ miles. _____ kilometers.

The legend on a map indicates that each inch equals 25 miles. Show mathematical computation in the space to the right.

4. Two inches on the map equals _____ miles. _____ kilometers.

5. Five inches on the map equals _____ miles. _____ kilometers.

6. Ten inches on the map equals _____ miles. _____ kilometers.

The legend on a map indicates that each inch equals seven miles. Show mathematical computation in the space to the right. Round to the nearest kilometer.

7. Two inches on the map equals _____ miles. _____ kilometers.

8. Five inches on the map equals _____ miles. _____ kilometers.

9. Ten inches on the map equals _____ miles. _____ kilometers.

Name _____ Date _____

Using a Map Legend

The legend below shows information that might be found on a map. Refer to the legend and answer the questions that follow.

LEGEND

🛡72 Interstate Highway	⊥ Historic Site	⛪ Church
★ State Capital	✪ National Capital	++++++ Railroad
∿ River	Marshland	⋈ Bridge
⋀ ⋀ Mountains	Scale: One inch equals ten miles	

Draw the legend symbol for:

1. An interstate highway.

2. A historic site.

3. A state capital.

4. A national capital.

5. A major river.

6. A marshland area.

7. On each line below, start at point "A," measure to the right the appropriate length, and place a slash where needed to portray the designated miles. (Refer to the map legend above to determine the scale).

   a. 10 miles

   A
   |_____

   b. 20 miles

   A
   |_____

   c. 40 miles

   A
   |_____

   d. 45 miles

   A
   |_____

   e. 50 miles

   A
   |_____

Name _____ Date _____

Learning More About Map Scale

In the previous exercises you have learned to read a map legend to determine how many miles on the earth are represented by the scale on the map. Sometimes the scale is listed as a **ratio** rather than as a statement.

Examples of scale definitions:

Statement definition: One inch equals one hundred miles.

Diagram definition: 0   100 miles   200 miles   300 miles

Ratio definition: 1/100
This ratio is read as "one mile on the map equals 100 miles on the earth.

Complete the following activity. Write a ratio scale for each of the following scale statements.

1. One inch equals fifty miles. _____

2. One inch equals five hundred miles. _____

3. One inch equals one thousand miles. _____

4. One inch equals twenty-five miles. _____

5. One inch equals five miles. _____

Write a statement scale for each of the following ratios.

6. 1/10 _____

7. 1/500 _____

8. 1/5 _____

9. 1/80 _____

10. 1/1.5 _____

Name _____ Date _____

State Map Exercise

For the next exercise it will be necessary to have a map of the state in which you live. Refer to the map and answer the following questions.

1. The scale of the map is _____ equals _____.

2. In the space to the right, draw the symbol for an interstate highway.

3. In the space below, list and draw the symbols for the various kinds of information found in the legend.

Comparing Globes and Maps

Name_____ Date_____

Maps are valuable tools. However, maps are **flat** surfaces that try to represent the round Earth. Maps often distort areas on Earth's surface.

Diagram 1
Regions A and B on a Circular Surface

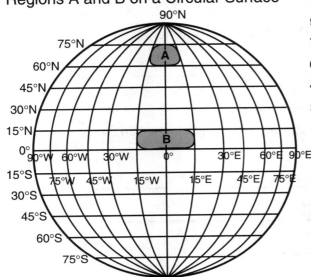

Diagram 2
Regions A and B on a Flat Surface

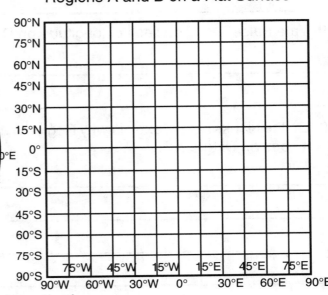

Refer to Diagram 1 and answer the following questions.

1. Region A is located between the longitude lines _____ and _____.

2. Region A is located between the latitude lines _____ and _____.

3. Region B is located between the longitude lines _____ and _____.

4. Region B is located between the latitude lines _____ and _____.

Diagram 2 is the same as Diagram 1, except that Diagram 2 has been drawn as a rectangle rather than as a circular figure. The lines of longitude and latitude are the same on both diagrams.

5. Using the longitude and latitude locations from Diagram 1, draw Regions A and B in the same locations on Diagram 2.

6. Region A on Diagram 2 appears (the same size as/larger than/smaller than) it does on Diagram 1.

7. Region B on Diagram 2 appears (the same size as/larger than/smaller than) it does on Diagram 1.

Name_____ Date _____

Answer the following questions as true or false. If false, explain why the statement is false on the blanks below the question.

8. True/False   The lines of latitude on Diagrams 1 and 2 are parallel.

_____

_____

9. True/False   The lines of longitude on Diagram 1 are parallel.

_____

_____

10. On the blanks below, explain why Region A appears so much larger on Diagram 2 than it does on Diagram 1.

_____

_____

_____

_____

_____

11. On the blanks below, explain why Region B appears approximately the same size on Diagrams 1 and 2.

_____

_____

_____

_____

_____

Name_____ Date _____

Flat Maps and Round Globes

A copy of Map I and a globe will be needed to complete the following exercise.

Circle the correct answer for each statement below.

1. On Map I the size (area) of Greenland appears to be (larger/smaller) than Australia.

2. On Map I the size (area) of Greenland appears to be (larger/smaller) than Mexico.

Refer to the globe and circle the correct answer for each statement below.

3. In size (area), Greenland appears to be (larger than/smaller than/the same size as) Australia.

4. In size (area), Greenland appears to be (larger than/smaller than/the same size as) Mexico.

Refer to Map I and answer the following. The vertical lines on Map I are lines of longitude. These are the lines labeled 0°, 15°E, 30°E, 45°E, 60°E, 75°E, 90°E, and 180° and 0°, 15°W, 30°W, 45°W, 60°W, 75°W, 90°W, and 180°.

5. Trace over each of the above lines beginning at the bottom of Map I and ending at the top of the map. Example: place the point of your pencil on 0° (Prime Meridian) at the bottom of the map, trace up the Prime Meridian, and end at the top of the map.

6. On Map I the lines of longitude (meet/do not meet).

Refer to the globe and answer the following.

7. The lines of longitude on the globe (meet/do not meet) at the North Pole.

8. Determine if the following statements are possible explanations for Greenland appearing much larger on the map than on the globe by underlining True or False.

    a. True/False   The lines of longitude on the globe meet at the poles, but the lines remain parallel on the map.

    b. True/False   The map shows that a degree of longitude equals the same distance at all locations.

    c. True/False   On a globe, the distance in miles for each degree between lines of longitude is greater near the equator than it is near the poles.

    d. True/False   The map is a flat surface, and the globe is a round surface. When Greenland is placed on a flat surface, the shape is distorted more than regions nearer the equator.

Understanding Latitude and Longitude
Teacher-Led Inquiry Session

To the Teacher: Students often have a difficult time understanding location using longitude and latitude. An understanding of rectangular coordinate systems and location activities using a grid will help students develop the prerequisite understanding necessary for mastering longitude and latitude.

Inquiry session:

It is important to develop an understanding of how latitude and longitude are used to locate points on the surface of the earth. To introduce students to the activities in this book, use a round ball that you can mark on, preferably a large ball the size of a basketball. It is important that a dot, cross, or other mark placed on the ball could not be located simply by description, so there should be no writing or lines on the ball.

Mark a spot on the ball that all students can see. Ask students the following questions.

1. Do you see the point I have marked on the ball?

2. Can anyone tell me where the point is located?

3. Place another point here (new point). Can you tell me where this new point is located?

4. Place the ball out of sight of the students. Have a student come up and mark a point on the ball. Have the student tell the class where the point has been placed.

5. Place students in groups and tell them they have ten minutes to come up with ways that the points placed on the ball can be located so that others can find the points using the system they develop.

Bring class together:

1. Draw a square on the board or overhead. Place a dot on the square that is not in the center of the square. Have students discuss how the location of the dot might be described to someone who could not see the paper. Ask them if they know of a way to precisely locate the dot so instructions could be given to another person and the other person could locate a dot precisely at the same point on a blank paper.

2. Have a square sheet of paper prepared for each student. Have a dot located on the paper that is not in the center of the paper. Send students back into groups for ten minutes to explore ways they might develop to precisely locate the dot. When the ten minutes are up, let students explain what they have determined.

12

3. Introduce a globe to the class so that students can see where you are pointing. Point to a spot in the Pacific Ocean that is not near any island or land. Pick a spot where a line of longitude and latitude cross. Do not call the lines of latitude and longitude to the attention of the students.

4. Tell the students that a ship is located at the place where you are pointing and the ship is experiencing difficulty. To save the ship, help must arrive within the next three hours. Planes are available at another location that can reach the ship in three hours if the planes fly at top speed. Therefore, it is necessary that the planes know exactly where the ship is located so that no time is wasted searching for the ship.

5. Ask students to show how the systems they developed could be used to accurately locate the ship. Help the students see the flaws or possibilities for success in the systems they have developed.

Place the students in the following situation:

Each student is the radio operator on the ship. The captain instructs the radio operator to contact the planes and give them a precise location of the ship so that the planes can locate and save the ship.

1. Guide students in a discussion of this problem. Let students explain how they would solve the problem. Why might their solution work? Is their solution a guess, or do they have reasons for their suggested answers? Leave the suggested solutions as possibilities that will be revisited later.

2. Place the words *longitude* and *latitude* on the board. Ask students if anyone knows what these words mean. Write the answers suggested by the students on the board. Have students tell why they think their answer is possibly correct. Where did they get the information? Is it a guess? End the discussion by indicating that in the upcoming lessons they will be learning more about these two words. It is not necessary to determine the correct answer at this point.

Name_____ Date _____

Using a Rectangular Coordinate System to Understand Longitude and Latitude: Dividing a Rectangle Into Quadrants

Refer to the rectangle below and complete the activity that follows.

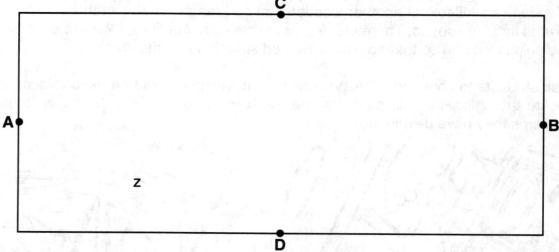

1. On the line below, describe where the letter "z" is located on the rectangle.

_____

2. Compare your answer with the answers given by others in your class.
3. Draw a line from "A" to "B."
4. Draw a line from "C" to "D."

   The rectangle is now divided into four parts or **quadrants**.

5. Begin in the quadrant in the upper right corner of the rectangle. Place a "I" in the upper left corner of this quadrant.
6. Move to the quadrant in the upper left side of the rectangle. Place a "II" in the upper left corner of this quadrant.
7. Move to the quadrant in the lower left side of the rectangle. Place a "III" in the upper left corner of this quadrant.
8. Move to the quadrant in the lower right side of the rectangle. Place a "IV" in the upper left corner of this quadrant.

   You now have four quadrants identified as Quadrants I, II, III, and IV.

9. On the line below, tell where the letter "z" is located on the rectangle.

_____

10. Compare your answer with others in your class.

Name _____ Date _____

Developing a Rectangular Coordinate System

In learning about longitude and latitude you are learning how places are located on the surface of the earth. The activity that follows will help you locate points using a rectangular coordinate system. You will also learn that longitude and latitude are used in a similar manner to locate places on the surface of the earth.

Refer to the rectangular coordinate system below and complete the activity that follows.

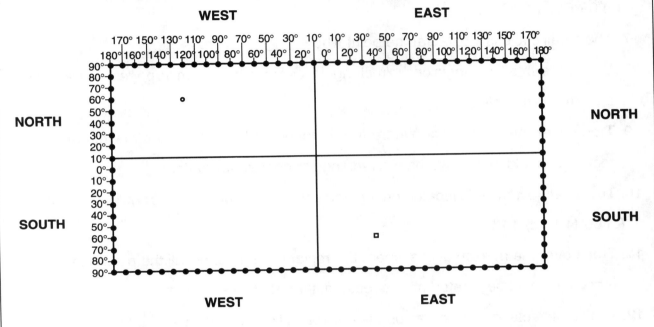

1. Connect the dots along the left and right sides of the rectangle to make a series of horizontal lines on the graph. The first one has been completed to connect the point 10°N on the left with 10°N on the right.

2. Connect the dots at the top and bottom of the rectangle to make a series of vertical lines on the graph. The first one has been completed to connect the point 10°W at the top to 10°W at the bottom.

   If you have completed the above activity correctly, you should have **horizontal** lines representing 0° to 90°N and 0° to 90°S. **Vertical** lines should represent 0° to 180° to the east and 0° to 180° west. Check with your teacher to make sure you have accurately completed this part of the activity before continuing.

Locate the small circle on the rectangular coordinate system. Trace over the circle.

3. Trace over the vertical line where the circle is to show all the places the circle could be located on the rectangular coordinate system.

　　　　15

Name _____ Date _____

4. The small circle is located on the vertical line that locates   (a) 60° W   (b) 120°W

    (c) 60°E   (d) 120°E.

5. Trace over the horizontal line where the circle is to show all the places the circle could

    be located on the rectangular coordinate system.

6. The small circle is located on the horizontal line that locates   (a) 60°N   (b)120°W

    (c) 60°E   (d) 120°E.

7. The small circle is located at the point where _____ °N crosses _____°W.

8. Locate the small rectangle on the rectangular coordinate system on page 15. Trace over

    the small rectangle.

9. Trace over the vertical line where the rectangle is to show all the places the small

    rectangle could be located on the rectangular coordinate system.

10. The small rectangle is located on the vertical line that locates   (a) 60°S   (b) 40°W

    (c) 60°N   (d) 40°E.

11. Trace over the horizontal line where the rectangle is to show all the places the small

    rectangle could be located on the rectangular coordinate system.

12. The small rectangle is located on the horizontal line that locates   (a) 60°S (b) 40°W

    (c) 60°N   (d) 40°E.

13. The small rectangle is located at the point where _____ °S crosses _____ °E.

Place a dot to locate the point on the rectangular coordinate system on page 15 for each
of the coordinates below.

14. 20°N, 10°E   15. 80°S, 100°E

16. 10°S, 90°W   17. 50°N, 30°E

18. 30°S, 140°W   19. 0°, 50°E

20. 70°S, 0°

Name _____ Date _____

Learning About Latitude and Longitude
Facts about Latitude

- Latitude measures distance north or south from the equator.

- Lines of latitude are all parallel.

- The equator marks 0° latitude.

- The equator is the only line of latitude that is a Great Circle.

- Latitude is measured in degrees. Latitude is measured from 0° to 90° north or south from the equator.

- The North Pole is 90°N latitude.

- The South Pole is 90°S latitude.

Refer to Diagram 3 to complete the activity below.

Diagram 3

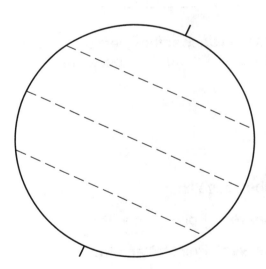

1. Draw a line over the line on Diagram 3 that represents the equator.

2. Place the symbol 0° in three places on the line that marks the equator.

3. Place the symbol 90°N on the point that represents the North Pole.

4. Place the symbol 90°S on the point that represents the South Pole.

Name _____ Date _____

Latitude lines are parallel lines. Refer to Diagram 4 and complete the activity below.

Diagram 4

Line A

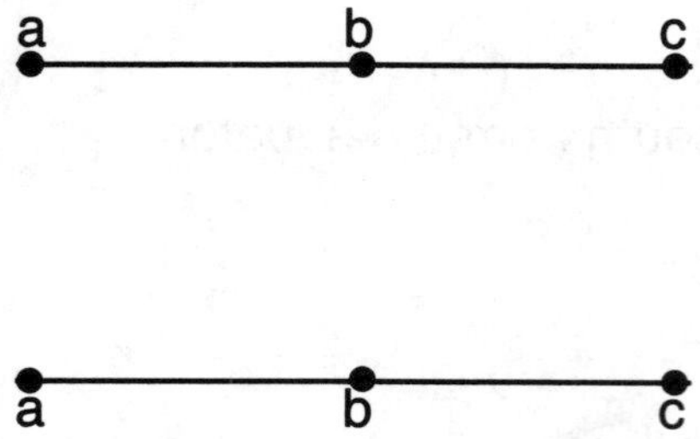

a   b   c

Line B

a   b   c

5. Measure the distance from "a" to "a." The distance is _____ inch(es).

6. Measure the distance from "b" to "b." The distance is _____ inch(es).

7. Measure the distance from "c" to "c." The distance is _____ inch(es).

   Lines that are **parallel** never cross. The lines are always the same distance apart.

8. Line A and Line B are parallel because _____

_____ .

9. Lines of latitude are _____ lines because they never _____ .

Follow the instructions, and then answer the questions that follow. Connect point "a" to "b" below; then connect point "c" to "d"; then connect point "e" to "f."

   a ●   ● b
   c ●   ● d
   e ●   ● f

10. The length of each of the above lines is _____ inches.

11. The vertical distance between Point "a" and Point "c" is _____ inch.

12. The vertical distance between Point "c" and Point "e" is _____ inch.

13. The vertical distance between Point "d" and Point "f" is _____ inch.

14. True/False.   The above three lines are parallel.

15. In the space below tell why line a—b is parallel to line e—f and line c—d.

_____

_____

Name _____ Date _____

Great Circles and Latitude

A **Great Circle** is a circle on the surface of the earth that divides the earth into two equal halves. If the earth could be sliced along the circle, the earth would be in two equal halves.

Refer to a globe and answer the following questions.

1. Locate the parallel lines on the globe. All of these lines are

   _____ on the globe. The largest circle is the

   equator.

2. Each of the parallel lines is a circle whose circumference gets smaller as the lines of

   latitude get closer to the _____ and _____ Poles.

3. Which line of latitude divides the earth into two equal halves? _____

4. This line is _____° latitude.

5. This line is a _____ Circle.

Fill in the blanks using the terms below:

    north   **parallel**   **equator**   **Great Circle**   **south**   **90**

6. The equator is the only line of latitude that is a _____ _____.

7. Latitude measures distance [circle one]   (a) north and south   (b) east and west

   from the equator.

8. In degrees, the distance from the equator to the North Pole is _____°.

9. In degrees, the distance from the equator to the South Pole is _____°.

10. Latitude lines are _____ lines that measure distance _____ and

    _____ from the equator.

Name_____ Date _____

Facts About Longitude

Nations have agreed that the Prime Meridian is the selected point from which longitude will be measured. The Prime Meridian is 0° longitude. Like all lines of longitude, the Prime Meridian is an imaginary line that runs from the North Pole to the South Pole. The Prime Meridian runs through Greenwich, England.

The Prime Meridian is the dividing line for the Eastern and Western Hemispheres. Everything from the Prime Meridian east to 180° is the Eastern Hemisphere. Everything from the Prime Meridian west to 180° is the Western Hemisphere.

Facts About Longitude

- All lines of longitude are Great Circles.

- All lines of longitude meet at the North and South Poles.

- Lines of longitude are not parallel because they meet at the poles.

- Lines of longitude measure distance east and west of the Prime Meridian.

- The International Date Line is 180° longitude; it is neither east nor west.

- The length of a degree of longitude is approximately 69 miles near the equator.

- The length of a degree of longitude gradually decreases as it nears the poles. At 60°N latitude, a degree of longitude is approximately 35 miles. At the poles, the value of a degree of longitude is 0.

Complete the following on Diagram 5 on page 21.

1. Trace over the line on Diagram 5 that represents the equator.

2. Place the symbol 0° in two places on the line that marks the Prime Meridian.

3. Place the symbol 90°N on the point that represents the North Pole.

4. Place the symbol 90°S on the point that represents the South Pole.

Name _____ Date _____

Refer to Diagram 5 to complete the next activity. The diagram represents that part of the globe between 10°W and 10°E longitude.

Diagram 5

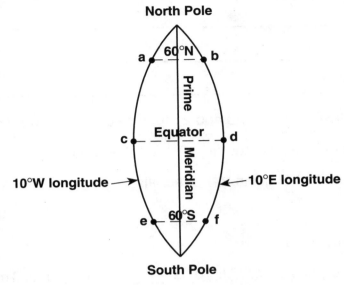

5. The distance from Point "a" to Point "b" is _____ degrees of longitude.

6. The distance from Point "c" to Point "d" is _____ degrees of longitude.

7. The distance from Point "e" to Point "f" is _____ degrees of longitude.

Note: All three lines, "a—b," "c—d," and "e—f," measure the distance between 10°W and 10°E longitude. In each case, the distance in degrees is 20° longitude.

Use a ruler and measure the distance from "a" to "b," "c" to "d," and "e" to "f." Then answer the following questions.

8. Which line(s) is/are the longest? _____

9. Which line(s) is/are the shortest? _____

10. I have found that the distance, in degrees, between each line is (the same/different).

11. I have found that the distance measured by a ruler is longer for line(s):

    (a—b, c—d, e—f).

12. I have found that the distance measured by a ruler is shorter for line(s):

    (a—b, c—d, e—f).

21

Name_____ Date _____

13. Explain why the distance measured by a ruler is longer for line "a—b" than for lines "c—d" and "e—f."

_____

_____

_____

Refer to the information on pages 20 and 21 to answer the following questions.

14. A degree of longitude along lines "a—b" and "e—f" equals _____ miles.

15. A degree of longitude along line "c—d" equals _____ miles.

Solve the following problems.

16. The distance in degrees from "a" to "b" is _____° longitude. The distance in miles from "a" to "b" is_____ miles.

17. The distance in degrees from "c" to "d" is_____° longitude. The distance in miles from "c" to "d" is _____ miles.

18. The distance in degrees from "e" to "f" is _____° longitude. The distance in miles from "e" to "f" is _____ miles.

Name _____ Date _____

Great Circles and Longitude

A **Great Circle** is a circle on the surface of the earth that divides the earth into two equal halves. If the earth could be sliced along the circle, the earth would be in two equal halves.

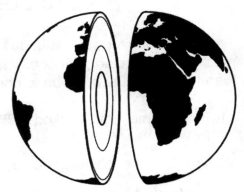

Refer to a globe and answer the following question.

1. True/False.   All lines of longitude are Great Circles.

Use these terms to fill in the blanks where needed in the exercise below.

east   **180**   **west**   **meet**

2. Longitude lines measure distance _____ or _____ of the Prime Meridian.

3. If you begin at the Prime Meridian and travel west like you were going to circle the earth and you stop at the International Date Line, you will have traveled   (a) 1/2   (b) 3/4   (c) 2/3   of the circle.

4. If you begin at the Prime Meridian and travel east like you were going to circle the earth and you stop at the International Date Line, you will have traveled   (a) 1/2   (b) 3/4   (c) 2/3   of the circle.

5. In degrees, the distance from the Prime Meridian west to the International Date Line is _____°.

6. In degrees, the distance from the Prime Meridian east to the International Date Line is _____°.

7. Longitude lines are not parallel because they _____ at the North and South Poles.

Name_____ Date _____

How Latitude and Longitude
Help to Locate Places on the Earth

The longitude and latitude system for locating points on the surface of the earth works much like the rectangular coordinate activity you completed on pages 15 and 16. Refer to Map I and an atlas or globe to complete the following activity.

1. Find the meridian marked 15°W and trace over the line from the North Pole to the South Pole.

2. Which of the following bodies of water are crossed by the 15°W longitude line?

North Atlantic Ocean	**Indian Ocean**
South Atlantic Ocean	**Pacific Ocean**

3. Which of the following continents are crossed by the 15°W longitude line?

Asia	**Europe**	**Africa**
North America	**South America**	**Antarctica**

4. Which of the following countries are crossed by the 15°W longitude line?

Ireland	**Iceland**	**United States**	**Senegal**
Gambia	**Germany**	**Western Sahara**	**Mauritania**

5. Which of the following hemispheres are crossed by the 15°W longitude line?

Northern	**Southern**	**Eastern**	**Western**

6. Find the latitude line marked 15°N and trace over the entire 15°N line of latitude.

7. Which of the following bodies of water are crossed by the 15°N latitude line?

North Atlantic Ocean	**Arabian Sea**
Pacific Ocean	**South Atlantic Ocean**

8. Which of the following continents are crossed by the 15°N line of latitude?

North America	**Europe**	**Asia**
Africa	**Australia**	**South America**

9. Which of the following countries are crossed by the 15°N latitude line?

Honduras	**Panama**	**India**	**Chad**
The Philippines	**China**	**Vietnam**	**Senegal**

Name _____ Date _____

10. Which of the following hemispheres are crossed by the 15°N latitude line?

Northern   **Southern**   **Eastern**   **Western**

11. Find the meridian marked 15°E longitude and trace over the line from the North Pole to the South Pole.

12. Which of the following bodies of water are crossed by the 15°E longitude line?

Baltic Sea   **Arctic Ocean**

Pacific Ocean   **Mediterranean Sea**

13. Which of the following continents are crossed by the 15°E longitude line?

Asia   **Europe**   **North America**

Australia   **Africa**   **Antarctica**

14. Which of the following countries are crossed by the 15°E longitude line?

Turkey   **Italy**   **Sweden**   **Brazil**

Libya   **France**   **Chad**   **Angola**

15. Which of the following hemispheres are crossed by the 15°E longitude line?

Northern   **Southern**   **Eastern**   **Western**

16. Find the latitude line marked 15°S and trace over the entire 15°S line of latitude.

17. Which of the following bodies of water are crossed by the 15°S latitude line?

North Atlantic Ocean   **Indian Ocean**

Pacific Ocean   **South Atlantic Ocean**

18. Which of the following continents are crossed by the 15°S latitude line?

South America   **North America**   **Europe**

Asia   **Australia**   **Africa**

19. Which of the following countries are crossed by the 15°S latitude line?

Mozambique   **Australia**   **Angola**   **Venezuela**

Peru   **Mexico**   **Brazil**   **Bolivia**

20. Which of the following hemispheres are crossed by the 15°S latitude line?

Northern   **Southern**   **Eastern**   **Western**

Name_____ Date _____

Solve the following:

21. An airplane crew radios that it is having difficulty and needs help. However, the only part of the message that is received is "location 60°E." On the blanks below, list some of the possible locations in which the plane might be found.

_____

_____

_____

_____

22. An airplane crew radios that it is having difficulty and needs help. However, the only part of the message that is received is "location 60°W." On the blanks below, list some of the possible locations in which the plane might be found.

_____

_____

_____

_____

_____

Name _____ Date _____

Measuring Degrees of Longitude

Diagram 6 below is looking at the earth that has been cut in half at the equator. Point A is the center of the earth. 0° represents the Prime Meridian on the surface of the earth. 90°W and 90°E are points where these lines of longitude are 90° from the Prime Meridian. The point marking 180° is 180° longitude (International Date Line). This point is 180° from the Prime Meridian. All lines of longitude are angles from 0° to 180°. If you draw a line from the center of the earth to the Prime Meridian and a line from the center of the earth to the selected line of longitude and then measure that angle, that gives you a measurement in degrees from 0 to 180.

Diagram 6

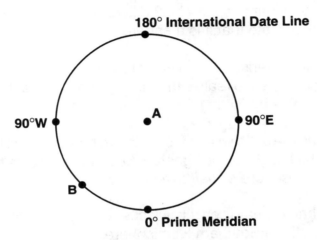

Use Diagram 6 and a protractor to complete the following.

1. Draw a line from Point A to the point where 90°W touches the surface of the earth.

2. Draw a line from Point A to the point where 0° touches the surface of the earth.

3. Measure the angle formed by these two lines with a protractor.

4. Which of the following is the angle formed from #1 and #2?

    (a) 45°   (b) 60°   (c) 90°   (d) 180°

5. Draw a line from Point A to the point where 90°E touches the surface of the earth.

6. Draw a line from Point A to the point where 0° touches the surface of the earth.

7. Measure the angle formed by these two lines.

8. Which of the following is the angle formed from #5 and #6?

    (a) 45°   (b) 60°   (c) 90°   (d) 180°

9. In questions #4 and #8, the angle formed is which of the following?

    (a) right   (b) obtuse (c) straight (d) oblique

10. Draw a line from Point A to Point B on the surface of the earth.

11. What is the angle formed by the lines from Point A to B and Point A to 0°?

    (a) 45°   (b) 90°   (c) 180°

Spheres and Hemispheres
Teacher-Led Inquiry Session

To the Teacher: Write the term *sphere* on the board or overhead. Use questions like the following to initiate discussion.

1. Who can pronounce the word? What sound do the letters "ph" make? Place some words like *phone, phonics,* and *photo* on the board or overhead and call attention to the fact that the letters "ph" always make the "f" sound when pronouncing the words.

2. Does anyone know what a "sphere" is? (Have two tennis or ping pong balls available.) Hold one up and indicate that it is a sphere.

3. What are the characteristics of a sphere? Write characteristics on the board or overhead. Students need to realize that an important characteristic is that a sphere can be divided into halves by cutting through the center.

4. Draw a line around the ball that divides it into two halves. Have the students discuss how each half of the ball might be designated. Lead the students to the idea that each half of the ball is a *hemi*sphere or *half* of a sphere.

5. Hold the ball so that one half is on top. Discuss calling this half the Northern Hemisphere and the bottom half the Southern Hemisphere.

6. Now, hold the second ball with the dividing line running from top to bottom. Discuss how the two halves might be designated since the Northern and Southern Hemispheres were used on the first ball. The discussion should determine that on the second ball the halves could be designated as the Western and Eastern Hemispheres.

7. Relate the above to a globe and the halves of the earth north and south of the equator and east and west of the Prime Meridian. Identify the Northern, Southern, Eastern, and Western Hemispheres.

8. Transfer the hemisphere understanding to locating the hemispheres on a wall map.

Name _____ Date _____

Reviewing Latitude and Longitude 1

Refer to Diagram 7 and Diagram 8 below to answer the following questions.

Diagram 7

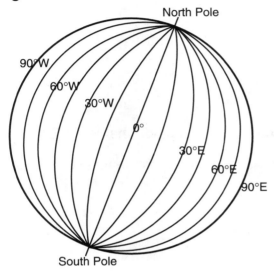

Diagram 8

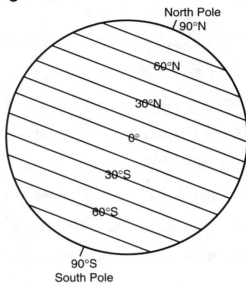

Circle the correct answers or fill in the blanks.

1. In Diagram 7 the lines are   (a) lines of longitude   (b) lines of latitude.

2. In Diagram 8 the lines are   (a) lines of longitude   (b) lines of latitude.

3. In Diagram 7 the line representing 0° longitude is called the _____ _____ .

4. In Diagram 8 the line representing 0° latitude is called the _____ .

5. Locate 0° longitude on Diagram 7. Write the words **Prime Meridian** on this line.

6. Each of the lines of longitude on Diagram 7 extend from the _____ Pole to the _____ Pole.

7. Each of the lines of longitude on Diagram 7 is either _____ or _____ of the Prime Meridian.

8. The distance, in degrees, from the Prime Meridian to 90°E is   (a) 10   (b) 45   (c) 75   (d) 90   degrees.

9. The distance, in degrees, from the Prime Meridian to 90°W is   (a) 10   (b) 45   (c) 75   (d) 90   degrees.

Name _____ Date _____

10. The distance from 90°E to 90°W is   (a) 90   (b) 0   (c) 180   (d) 60   degrees.

11. Place letter "a" in six different places along the line of longitude that is 60°W.

12. The only statement that can be made about the locations of the letters "a" is that:

  (a) they are all east of the Prime Meridian.

  (b) they are all west of the Prime Meridian.

  (c) they are all north of the Prime Meridian.

  (d) they are all south of the Prime Meridian.

13. Place letter "b" in six different places along the line of longitude that is 60°E.

14. The only statement that can be made about the locations of the letters "b" is that:

  (a) they are all east of the Prime Meridian.

  (b) they are all west of the Prime Meridian.

  (c) they are all north of the Prime Meridian.

  (d) they are all south of the Prime Meridian.

15. Place the letter "c" in six different places along the line of latitude that is 30°S.

16. The only statement that can be made about the locations of the letters "c" is that:

  (a) they are all east of the equator.

  (b) they are all west of the equator.

  (c) they are all north of the equator.

  (d) they are all south of the equator.

Name _____ Date _____

Identifying Hemispheres

Refer to a copy of Map I and complete the following activity.

1. The continents located **totally** west of the Prime Meridian are:

    (a) North America and South America.

    (b) North America and Asia.

    (c) South America and Australia.

    (d) Africa and Asia.

2. The continents located **totally** east of the Prime Meridian are:

    (a) North America and South America.

    (b) North America and Asia.

    (c) Asia and Australia.

    (d) Africa and Asia.

3. The continents located **both** east and west of the Prime Meridian are:

    (a) North America and South America.

    (b) North America and Asia.

    (c) South America and Australia.

    (d) Africa and Europe.

4. The continents located **totally** north of the equator are:

    (a) North America and Africa.

    (b) North America and Europe.

    (c) Asia and Africa.

    (d) Europe and Australia.

5. The continents located **totally** south of the equator are:

    (a) South America and Africa.

    (b) Africa and Australia.

    (c) Australia and Antarctica.

    (d) South America and Asia.

Name _____ Date _____

6. The continents located **both** north and south of the equator are:

   (a) South America, Asia, and Africa.

   (b) Australia, Europe, and Africa.

   (c) Antarctica, Africa, and Asia.

   (d) Asia, North America, and Australia.

7. North America is located in the:

   (a) Eastern and Southern Hemispheres.

   (b) Northern and Western Hemispheres.

   (c) Northern and Eastern Hemispheres.

   (d) Western and Southern Hemispheres.

8. Australia is located in the:

   (a) Eastern and Southern Hemispheres.

   (b) Northern and Western Hemispheres.

   (c) Northern and Eastern Hemispheres.

   (d) Western and Southern Hemispheres.

9. Asia is located in the:

   (a) Eastern and Southern Hemispheres.

   (b) Northern and Western Hemispheres.

   (c) Northern and Eastern Hemispheres.

   (d) Western and Southern Hemispheres.

10. Africa is located in the:

   (a) Eastern, Western, and Southern Hemispheres.

   (b) Northern, Eastern, and Western Hemispheres.

   (c) Northern, Eastern, and Southern Hemispheres.

   (d) Western, Northern, Southern, and Eastern Hemispheres.

Name_____ Date _____

Locating Lines of Latitude and Longitude

Refer to a copy of Map I and complete the following activity.

1. Use a pencil or crayon and trace over the longitude line that marks 90°E.

2. Use a pencil or crayon and trace over the longitude line that marks 90°W.

3. The number of degrees of longitude between 90°E and 90°W is_____°.

4. Locate 15°E. Is there a 15°W?   yes   no

5. Locate 30°E. Is there a 30°W?   yes   no

6. Locate 45°W. Is there a 45°E?   yes   no

7. Locate 60°W. Is there a 60°E?   yes   no

8. The only line of longitude on Map I that does not have an east or west location is:

    (a) 60°   (b) 75°   (c) 180°   (d) 120°.

9. The distance from 180° to the Prime Meridian is   (a) 90°   (b) 120°   (c) 180°   (d) 60°.

10. Trace over the line of latitude that passes over Mexico, Florida, the Atlantic Ocean, Algeria, Egypt, Saudi Arabia, China, and the Pacific Ocean. This line of latitude is _____ ° north of the equator.

11. Trace over the line of latitude that passes over Chile, Argentina, the Atlantic Ocean, South Africa, the Indian Ocean, Australia, and the Pacific Ocean. This line of latitude is _____ ° south of the equator.

12. Trace over the line of latitude that passes over Canada, the Atlantic Ocean, Norway, Sweden, Russia, and the Pacific Ocean. This line of latitude is 60° _____ of the equator.

13. Circle the countries that are located between 30°W to 60°W longitude and between 0° and 30°S latitude.

Argentina	Chile	Brazil	Turkey	Mexico
Finland	Spain	Greenland	Paraguay	Bolivia

14. Circle the countries that are located between 30°E to 60°E longitude and between 0° and 30°N latitude.

Argentina	Saudi Arabia	Brazil	Turkey	Egypt
Finland	Spain	Israel		

Name_____ Date _____

Using Latitude and Longitude
to Locate Areas on a Map

Refer to the map below and answer the following questions.

1. The area on the map marked [hatched box] is located between _____° and _____° east of the Prime Meridian.

2. The area on the map marked [grid box] is located between _____° and _____° north of the equator.

3. The area on the map marked [hatched box] is located between _____° and _____° west of the Prime Meridian.

4. The area on the map marked [dotted box] is located between _____° and _____° south of the equator.

5. Color blue the area on the map that is between 30° and 60°N latitude.

6. Color green the area on the map that is between 30° and 60°W longitude.

7. Color yellow the area on the map that is between 30° and 60°S latitude.

8. Color red the area on the map that is between 30° and 60°E longitude.

9. Color purple the area that is between 60° and 90°N and is between 0° and 30°W.

10. Color orange the area that is between 60° and 90°S and is between 0° and 30°E.

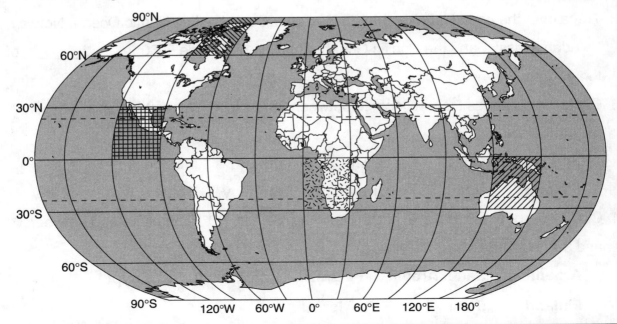

Name _____ Date _____

Latitude and Longitude Crossword Puzzle

Use the clues below to complete the crossword. Answers may be found in the material dealing with latitude and longitude.

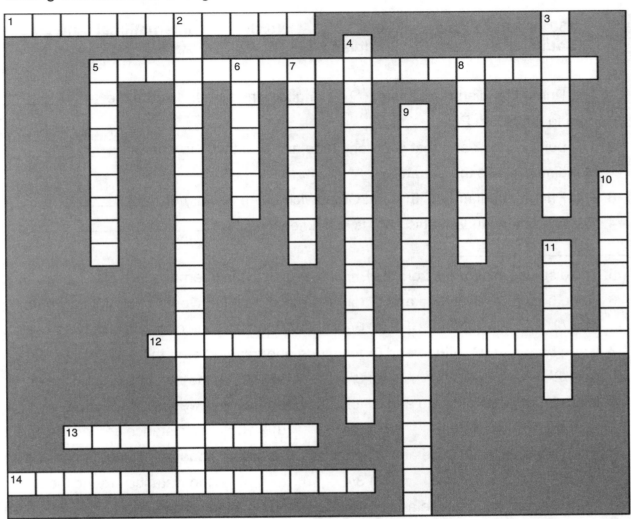

ACROSS

1. A line that divides the earth into two equal halves (two words)
5. All places on Earth south of the equator are in the _____ _____.
12. All places on Earth east from the Prime Meridian to 180° are in the _____ _____ .
13. Measures distance east and west from the Prime Meridian
14. The name given to 0° longitude (two words)

DOWN

2. Name given to 180° longitude line (three words)
3. Another name for lines of longitude
4. All places on Earth west from the Prime Meridian to 180° are in the _____ _____ .
5. Represents 90°S latitude (two words)
6. The name given to 0° latitude
7. Represents 90°N latitude (two words)
8. Another name for lines of latitude
9. All places on Earth north of the equator are in the _____ _____.
10. Measures distance north and south from the equator
11. Unit of longitude and latitude measurement

Name _____ Date _____

Reviewing Latitude and Longitude 2

Use a globe to complete the following activity. Choose from the following terms to complete the blanks.

180	**Prime**	**0**	**North**	**International Date Line**
South	**Japan**	**England**		

1. The Prime Meridian represents _____° longitude and extends from the _____ Pole to the South Pole.

2. The point on the earth that is 0° longitude and 0° latitude is where the_____ Meridian crosses the equator.

3. The Prime Meridian runs through Greenwich in the country of _____.

4. The line of longitude that is 180° is also known as the _____
_____ _____.

5. The distance in degrees from the Prime Meridian to the International Date Line is ____°.

6. If you began at 0° latitude and 0° longitude and traveled **west** to 90°W, you would be
(a) 1/2   (b) 1/4   (c) 3/4   (d) 1/10   the distance around the earth.

7. If you began at 0° latitude and 0° longitude and traveled **east** to 90°W, you would be
(a) 1/2   (b) 1/4   (c) 3/4   (d) 1/10   the distance around the earth.

8. If you began at 0° latitude and 0° longitude and traveled **west** to 180°, you would be
(a) 1/2   (b) 1/4   (c) 3/4   (d) 1/10   the distance around the earth.

9. If you began at 0° latitude and 0° longitude and traveled **east** to 180°W, you would be
(a) 1/2   (b) 1/4   (c) 3/4   (d) 1/10   the distance around the earth.

10. If you began at 0° latitude and 0° longitude and traveled **north** to 90°N, you would be
(a) 1/2   (b) 1/4   (c) 3/4   (d) 1/10   the distance around the earth.

11. If you began at 0° latitude and 0° longitude and traveled **south** to 90°S, you would be
(a) 1/2   (b) 1/4   (c) 3/4   (d) 1/10   the distance around the earth.

12. If you began at 0° latitude and 0° longitude and traveled to 90°N and then went south along 180° longitude to 0° latitude, you would be   (a) 1/2   (b) 1/4   (c) 3/4   (d) 1/10 the distance around the earth from where you started.

13. If you began at 0° latitude and 0° longitude and traveled to 90°S and then went north along 180° longitude to 0° latitude, you would be   (a) 1/2   (b) 1/4   (c) 3/4   (d) 1/10 the distance around the earth from where you started.

Name _____ Date _____

14. Place a plus (+) sign by the statements that are true for latitude.

_____ (a) Latitude lines are all Great Circles.

_____ (b) The only line of latitude that is a Great Circle is the equator.

_____ (c) Latitude measures distance north or south from the equator.

_____ (d) The highest degrees of latitude are 90°N and 90°S.

15. Place a plus (+) sign by the statements that are true for longitude.

_____ (a) Longitude lines meet at the poles.

_____ (b) Longitude lines meet at the equator.

_____ (c) All lines of longitude are Great Circles.

_____ (d) The highest degree of longitude is 180°.

16. Each of the statements below is true for either longitude or latitude. Place each of the letters for the statements under the column labeled "Longitude" or "Latitude."

(a) Measures distance north or south from the equator.

(b) Is measured from the Prime Meridian.

(c) Is measured from the equator.

(d) Only 0° is a Great Circle.

(e) All lines are Great Circles.

(f) Measurements are from 0° to 90° north or south.

(g) Measurements are from 0° to 180° east or west.

(h) Measures distance east or west from the Prime Meridian.

(i) Lines are parallel.

(j) Lines meet at the poles.

Longitude	**Latitude**
_____	_____
_____	_____

Name_____ Date _____

Where on Earth is This Location?

Now that you have learned about latitude and longitude, let's locate places on Earth using coordinates. First, locate the line of latitude indicated, and then follow that line until it meets the line of longitude indicated. The point where the two lines meet is the point indicated by the coordinates.

Place a dot on Map II at each set of latitude and longitude coordinates.

1. 60°N, 75°E   2. 30°S, 135°W   3. 0°, 0°

4. 75°N, 0°   5. 75°S, 0°   6. 0°, 150°W

7. 0°, 150°E   8. 45°N, 45°E   9. 45°S, 45°W

10. 75°N, 180°   11. 75°S, 180°

Where is This City Located?

Match the following cities with their latitude and longitude coordinates. Place the letter of the coordinates in Column B that most nearly locates the city on the blank next to that city in Column A. Refer to Map II, an atlas, or a globe to complete the activity.

Column A	Column B
_____ 1. Rio de Janeiro	A. 35°S, 149°E
_____ 2. Vancouver	B. 33°S, 18°E
_____ 3. Canberra	C. 45°N, 75°W
_____ 4. Shanghai	D. 51°N, 0°
_____ 5. Dakar	E. 31°N, 121°E
_____ 6. Anchorage	F. 22°S, 43°W
_____ 7. Ottawa	G. 30°N, 31°E
_____ 8. Manila	H. 61°N, 149°W
_____ 9. London	I. 19°N, 73°E
_____ 10. Los Angeles	J. 15°N, 17°W
_____ 11. Bombay	K. 34°S, 58°W
_____ 12. Cairo	L. 41°N, 87°W
_____ 13. Cape Town	M. 49°N, 123°W
_____ 14. Buenos Aires	N. 14°N, 121°E
_____ 15. Chicago	O. 34°N, 118°W

Name _____ Date _____

Converting Degrees of Latitude and Longitude to Miles and Kilometers

Longitude and latitude are measured in **degrees**, **minutes**, and **seconds**. Three hundred sixty degrees make up a circle, 60 minutes make up one degree, and 60 seconds make up one minute.

Degrees in longitude and latitude can be converted into miles or kilometers. Let's use the equator as an example.

The equator is a circle around the earth. A circle has 360°. It is known that the distance in miles around the earth at the equator is approximately 24,900 miles. Each degree of longitude measured east or west of the Prime Meridian at the equator equals approximately 69 miles. A kilometer is 0.621 of a mile. Another way of saying this is that each mile equals 1.6 kilometers.

Example: 100 miles x 1.6 = 160, so 100 miles equals 160 kilometers

So, if the equator is 24,900 miles long, we multiply 24,900 x 1.6 to get 39,840 km.

Change the miles in Column A to kilometers. Write the answer in Column B.

Column A   **Column B**

1.   100 miles   times 1.6 equals   _____ kilometers

2.   150 miles   times 1.6 equals   _____ kilometers

3.   200 miles   times 1.6 equals   _____ kilometers

4.   500 miles   times 1.6 equals   _____ kilometers

5.   1,000 miles   times 1.6 equals   _____ kilometers

To find how many miles someone travels along the equator, multiply 69 times the number of degrees of longitude traveled. Then convert the miles to kilometers.

6. You depart from 0° longitude and 0° latitude and travel west along the equator to 15°W longitude, 0° latitude. You have traveled (a)_____ °. The distance, in miles, traveled is (b)_____ miles. The distance, in kilometers, is (c)_____.

7. You depart from 0° longitude and 0° latitude and travel west along the equator to 90°W longitude, 0° latitude. You have traveled (a)_____ °. The distance, in miles, traveled is (b)_____ miles. The distance, in kilometers, is (c)_____.

Name _____ Date _____

8. You depart from 0° longitude and 0° latitude and travel east along the equator to 75°E longitude, 0° latitude. You have traveled   (a)_____°. The distance, in miles, traveled is (b) _____ miles. The distance, in kilometers, is (c) _____.

9. You depart from 0° longitude and 0° latitude and travel east along the equator to 150°E longitude, 0° latitude. You have traveled   (a)_____°. The distance, in miles, traveled is (b)_____ miles. The distance, in kilometers, is (c) _____.

10. You depart from 0° longitude and 0° latitude and travel east along the equator to 40°W longitude, 0° latitude. You have traveled   (a)_____°. The distance, in miles, traveled is (b)_____ miles. The distance, in kilometers, is (c)_____.

11. You depart from 0° longitude and 0° latitude and travel east along the equator to 180° longitude, 0° latitude. You have traveled   (a)_____°. The distance, in miles, traveled is (b)_____ miles. The distance, in kilometers, is (c) _____.

    You have traveled: (circle one)   (d) 1/3   (e) 1/2   (f) 1/4   (g) 1/8

    the distance around the earth at the equator.

40

Name _____ Date _____

Distance in Degrees and Miles/Kilometers
at Various Latitudes

The equator is the only line of latitude that is a Great Circle. However, all lines of latitude are circles consisting of 360°. Beginning at the equator and going north or south, each line of latitude is a circle that is smaller and smaller. The circles for latitudes 10°N and 10°S are smaller circles than the equator.

1. Each of the following circles represents a line of latitude that circles the earth in the Northern Hemisphere. This is the view of each line of latitude when looking down on the earth from a position over the North Pole. Place each of the bold latitudes on the circle that best represents the line of latitude.

50°N   60°N   10°N   70°N   30°N   40°N   20°N

a. 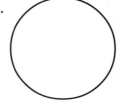   b. 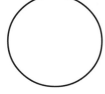   c. 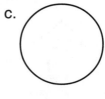   d.

e. ⃝   f. ⃝   g. ⃝

Indicate if the following statements are true or false. If the statement is false, make it true by rewriting the statement on the blank below each statement.

2. (T / F)   Each of the circles in the previous diagram has 360°.

_____

3. (T / F)   The diameter of each circle is the same.

_____

4. (T / F)   The circumference of each circle is the same.

_____

Name _____ Date _____

Each of the three circles below shows a line of latitude that circles the earth at three different latitudes in the Northern Hemisphere. Each line of latitude is a circle consisting of 360°.

On the earth, each degree of longitude at 10°N latitude equals 69 miles. Each degree of longitude at 30°N latitude represents 60 miles. Each degree of longitude at 60°N latitude represents 35 miles. The line on Circle A below represents 10°N latitude. The line on Circle B represents 30°N latitude. The line on Circle C represents 60°N latitude.

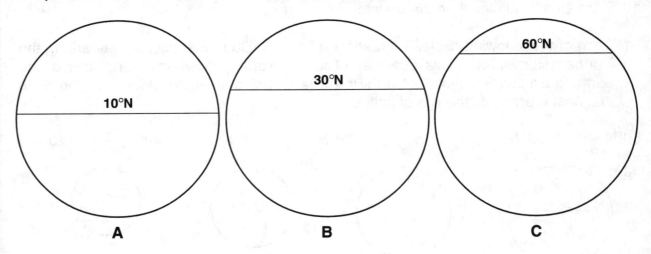

5. The distance around the earth on the line of latitude on Circle A is

(a) _____ miles or

(b) _____ kilometers.

6. The distance around the earth on the line of latitude on Circle B is

(a) _____ miles or

(b) _____ kilometers.

7. The distance around the earth on the line of latitude on Circle C is

(a) _____ miles or

(b) _____ kilometers.

Name_____ Date _____

Measuring Longitude and Latitude
in Miles and Kilometers

Two facts are important to understand about the lines of latitude and longitude.

First, let's look at latitude. The distance around the earth in miles or kilometers decreases at higher latitudes. For example, the distance around the earth at 60°N is 12,600 miles or 20,160 kilometers. The distance around the earth in miles at 20°N is 23,400 miles or 37,440 kilometers.

Second, let's look at longitude. The lines of longitude are farthest apart at the equator. The lines of longitude come closer together until they meet at the poles. Also, the lines of longitude are intersecting lines of latitude that circle the earth in smaller and smaller circles as the poles are approached. However, each of the circles of latitude is still 360°.

Example I:

The location is 0° latitude, 15°W longitude. Zero degrees latitude is a circle of 360° around the earth. The distance around the earth at 0° latitude is approximately 24,900 miles. To find the number of miles per degree, divide 24,900 by 360°. 24,900 ÷ 360° = 69 miles.

Problem: At 0° latitude, what is the distance (in miles) from the Prime Meridian to 15°W?

15° x 69 = 1,035   A ship located at 0°, 15°W is 1,035 miles from the Prime Meridian.

Example II:

The location is 30°N latitude, 15°W longitude. Thirty degrees north latitude is a circle of 360° around the earth. The distance around the earth at 30° latitude is 21,600 miles. To find the number of miles per degree, divide 21,600 by 360°. 21,600 ÷ 360° = 60 miles.

Problem: At 30°N latitude, what is the distance (in miles) from the Prime Meridian to 15°W?

15° x 60 = 900   A ship located at 30°N, 15°W is 900 miles from the Prime Meridian.

Example III:

The location is 60°N latitude, 15°W longitude. Sixty degrees north latitude is a circle of 360° around the earth. The distance around the earth at 60°N latitude is 12,600 miles. To find the number of miles per degree, divide 12,600 by 360°. 12,600 ÷ 360° = 35 miles.

Problem: At 60°N latitude, what is the distance (in miles) from the Prime Meridian to 15°W?

15° x 35 = 525   A ship located at 60°N, 15°W is 525 miles from the Prime Meridian.

Name _____ Date _____

Latitude:

To measure the distance north or south of the equator, take the degrees of latitude times 69 miles. If you start at the North Pole and go around the earth back to the North Pole, the distance is approximately 24,900 miles. 24,900 ÷ 360° = 69. Each degree of latitude equals 69 miles.

Table 1:

1° of longitude = 69 miles at 0° latitude
1° of longitude = 60 miles at 30° latitude
1° of longitude = 35 miles at 60° latitude

1° of latitude = 69 miles

Refer to an atlas and complete the following charts.

Chart I:

City	Latitude	Longitude	Miles from Equator	Miles from Prime Meridian
1. Quito, Ecuador	_____	_____	_____	_____
2. Cairo, Egypt	_____	_____	_____	_____
3. Oslo, Norway	_____	_____	_____	_____
4. Juneau, Alaska	_____	_____	_____	_____
5. Singapore	_____	_____	_____	_____
6. Shanghai, China	_____	_____	_____	_____
7. New Orleans, Louisiana	_____	_____	_____	_____
8. Jacksonville, Florida	_____	_____	_____	_____

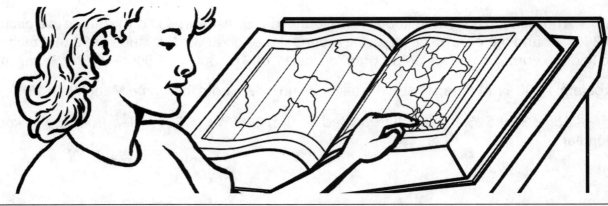

Name _____ Date _____

Convert from miles to kilometers to complete Chart II below. Round to the nearest kilometer.

Chart II:

City	Kilometers from Equator	Kilometers from Prime Meridian
1. Quito, Ecuador	_____	_____
2. Cairo, Egypt	_____	_____
3. Oslo, Norway	_____	_____
4. Juneau, Alaska	_____	_____
5. Singapore	_____	_____
6. Shanghai, China	_____	_____
7. New Orleans, Louisiana	_____	_____
8. Jacksonville, Florida	_____	_____

Refer to the previous charts to answer the following questions.

1. A ship is located at 30°N, 60°W. The distance of the ship from the Prime Meridian is

   _____ miles or_____ kilometers.

2. The distance of the ship from the equator is _____ miles or_____ kilometers.

3. An island is located at 0° latitude, 75°E longitude. The distance of the island from the

   Prime Meridian is _____ miles or_____ kilometers.

4. An island is located at 30°S, 135°W. The distance of the island from the Prime Meridian

   is _____ miles or_____ kilometers.

5. The distance of the island from the equator is _____ miles or_____ kilo-

   meters.

Name_____ Date _____

Latitude True/False

Answer each of the following statements as true (T) or false (F). If a statement is false, correct it and rewrite it as a true statement on the blank below each question.

_____ 1. The only line of latitude that is a Great Circle is the equator.

_____

_____ 2. All lines of latitude are circles of 180°.

_____

_____ 3. The distance around the earth is the same at different latitudes.

_____

_____ 4. A degree of longitude at 30°N latitude and 70°N latitude represents the same number of miles.

_____

_____ 5. All lines of latitude are parallel.

_____

_____ 6. The distances around the earth in degrees at 0°, 30°S, and 60°S are all 360°.

_____

_____ 7. The distance around the earth in miles is greater at 60°N than at 30°N.

_____

_____ 8. The distance around the earth in kilometers is less at 60°S than at 30°S.

_____

_____ 9. The North Pole represents 90°N latitude.

_____

_____ 10. Latitude extends from 0° to 90°N and from 0° to 90°W.

_____

_____ 11. If only the latitude location is known, then a location might be in either the Eastern or Western Hemisphere.

_____

Name _____ Date _____

Longitude True/False

Answer each of the following statements as true (T) or false (F). If a statement is false, correct it and rewrite it as a true statement on the blank below each question.

_____ 1. All lines of longitude are Great Circles.

_____

_____ 2. Lines of longitude extend from the North Pole to the South Pole.

_____

_____ 3. The equator is a line of longitude.

_____

_____ 4. Each line of longitude is parallel to another line of longitude.

_____

_____ 5. All lines of longitude meet at the North Pole and equator.

_____

_____ 6. Longitude measures distance east and west from the equator.

_____

_____ 7. The distance (in kilometers) between 10°E and 10°W at 10°N latitude is the same as it is at 60°N latitude.

_____

_____ 8. The Prime Meridian represents 0° longitude.

_____

_____ 9. The International Date Line represents 180° latitude.

_____

_____ 10. There is only one line of longitude that represents 180°.

_____

_____ 11. If only the longitude location is known, then a location might be in either the Northern or Southern Hemisphere.

_____

Name _____ Date _____

Review Exercise

Refer to a copy of Map I and complete the following exercise.

1. Begin at 0° latitude, 0° longitude and travel north 30°. Place a dot at this location. Now, from the dot, travel 120° east and place a dot at this location. Now, travel north 30° and place a dot at this location.

2. How many miles did you travel from 0°, 0° to the first dot? _____ miles

3. How many kilometers did you travel from 0°, 0° to the first dot? _____ km

4. How many miles did you travel from the first dot to the second dot? _____ miles

5. How many kilometers did you travel from the first dot to the second dot? _____ km

6. How many miles did you travel from the second dot to the final dot? _____ miles

7. How many kilometers did you travel from the second dot to the final dot? _____ km

8. Place a dot at 45°N, 120°W.

9. Place a dot at 30°N, 120°W.

10. Place a dot at 45°N, 75°W.

11. Place a dot at 30°N, 75°W.

12. Draw a line to connect the dots in 8, 9, 10, and 11.

13. Color in the region inside the dots.

14. What country is located mostly inside the region colored? _____

15. Place a dot at 15°S, 120°E.

16. Place a dot at 30°S, 120°E.

17. Place a dot at 15°S, 150°E.

18. Place a dot at 30°S, 150°E.

19. Draw a line to connect the dots in 15, 16, 17, and 18.

20. Color in the region inside the dots.

21. What country is located mostly inside the region colored? _____

A pilot is forced to bail out of her aircraft. She radios her location, but it is received as a garbled message. However, the rescue team is able to verify that the pilot is down somewhere inside the area bounded by these points: 15°S, 60°E; 15°S, 75°E; 30°S, 60°E; 30°S, 75°E.

22. Color in the region where the pilot might be located.

Name _____ Date _____

Place a dot on Map I for each of the latitudes and longitudes in the problems below. Then, change the latitude and longitude locations to the Southern and Western Hemispheres. Locate the new latitude and longitude with a dot on Map I, as well. The first one has been changed for you.

23. 75°N, 135°E   <u>75°S, 135°W</u>

24. 15°N, 150°E   _____

25. 30°N, 30°E   _____

26. 60°N, 45°E   _____

27. 10°N, 165°E   _____

28. 45°N, 90°E   _____

Each of the following latitude and longitude coordinates is in one of the nations listed. Locate the coordinates on Map I, an atlas, world map, or globe. Underline the correct nation from the four choices.

29. 4°N, 72°W   **Colombia**   **France**   **China**   **South Africa**

30. 10°S, 55°W   **Pakistan**   **Brazil**   **Iceland**   **New Zealand**

49

Name _____ Date _____

Latitude and Longitude Atlas Activities

Refer to a map of Europe in an atlas to complete the following.

1. Begin on the left side of the map and trace over 50°N latitude to 0° longitude with your finger. Trace 0° longitude north to the top of the map. Circle the following countries that are north of 50° latitude and west of 0° longitude.

   Ireland   France   Spain   Scotland

2. Begin on the left side of the map and trace over 50°N latitude to 10°E longitude with your finger. Trace 10°E longitude north to the top of the map. Circle the following countries that are north of 50° latitude and west of 10°E longitude.

   Ireland   Belgium   England   Denmark
   Poland   Italy   Northern Ireland

3. Begin on the left side of the map and trace over 45°N latitude to 15°E longitude with your finger. Trace 15°E longitude north to the top of the map. Circle the following countries that are located totally north of 45°N latitude and west of 15°E longitude.

   Germany   France   Austria   Denmark   Northern Ireland
   England   Wales   Ireland   Switzerland

4. Begin on the left side of the map and trace over 45°N latitude to 10°E longitude with your finger. Trace 10°E longitude south to the bottom of the map. Circle the following countries that are south of 45°N latitude and west of 10°E longitude.

   Belgium   Spain   England   Portugal   Northern Ireland

Refer to a map of North America in an atlas to complete the following.

5. Begin on the left side of the map and trace over 30°N latitude with your finger. Circle the following countries that have all or part of their territory located south of 30°N and between 90°W and 110°W.

   Guatemala Panama   Costa Rica Mexico   Cuba   United States

6. Begin on the left side of the map and trace over 30°N latitude with your finger. Circle the following countries that have all or part of their territory located south of 30°N and between 70°W and 90°W.

   Haiti   Panama   Nicaragua Mexico   Dominican Republic
   Jamaica   Cuba   Canada   United States

Name _____ Date _____

7. Begin at the bottom of the map and trace 90°W to the top of the map with your finger. Circle the countries that lie on 90°W.

Canada   **Panama**   **Honduras**   **Mexico**   **Dominican Republic**

Guatemala   **United States**   **Belize**

Refer to a map of Africa in an atlas to complete the following.

8. Begin on the left side of the map and trace over 0° latitude to 10°E longitude with your finger. Trace over 10°E up to the coast of the Mediterranean Sea. Circle the countries that are north of 0° latitude, and west of 10°E.

Nigeria   **Gambia**   **Angola**   **Liberia**   **South Africa**

Ghana   **Senegal**   **Sudan**   **Mali**   **Sierra Leone**

9. Begin at the top of the map and trace south over 0° longitude to 10°N latitude with your finger. Trace over 10°N west to the coast of Africa. Circle the nations that are north of 10°N and west of 0° longitude.

Kenya   **Mauritania**   **Morocco**   **Angola**   **Egypt**   **Sudan**

10. The African country with **all** of its territory located north of 20°N and east of 20°E is:

Libya   **Sudan**   **Egypt**   **Chad**

Refer to a map of Asia in an atlas to complete the following.

11. Begin on the left side of the map and trace over 45°N with your finger to the point where 45°N meets 75°E. Trace south over 75°E to the bottom of the map. Circle the countries that are located in the area south of 45°N and west of 75°E.

Turkey   **Iran**   **Saudi Arabia**   **Afghanistan**

Pakistan   **Iraq**   **Israel**

12. Begin on the left side of the map and trace over 15°N with your finger to the point where 15°N meets 120°E. Trace over 120°E to the bottom of the map. Circle the following countries located south of 15°N and west of 120°E.

Japan   **Malaysia**   **Indonesia**

Name_____ Date _____

Latitude and Longitude Practice Exercise 1

Refer to a copy of Map II to complete the following.

1. You are located at 22°S, 43°W. You fly to 35°S, 149°E. You stop for a day to enjoy the beach and some swimming. Then you fly to 55°N, 37°E, where you spend the day visiting the Kremlin. Finally, you travel to 45°N, 75°W to spend the summer. The cities you have visited are   (a) _____ , (b) _____ , (c) _____ , and (d) _____ .

2. You are located at 61°N, 149°W. You travel directly south from this location to 15°N and then east to 17°W. You then travel directly north to 31°N and turn east and travel to 121°E. In your travels, you were in the cities of   (a) _____ , (b) _____ , and (c) _____ .

3. You are in the city located at 22°S, 43°W. You leave the city and fly northeast to a city located at 40°N, 3°W, where you board a train bound for the city located at 49°N, 2°E. From this city you board a ship on the Seine River that is bound for a city located at 51°N, 0°, located on the Thames River. You traveled from the city of   (a)_____ to (b) _____ , then to   (c) _____ , and finally to (d)_____ .

4. You begin your trip at a city located at 41°N, 87°W, which is located on Lake Michigan. You board a plane and fly southeast to a city located at 15°N, 17°W near the Atlantic Ocean. Then you board a ship that sails southwest to a city located at 34°S, 58°W. The next day you fly east to a city located at 34°S, 18°E. You traveled from the city of (a) _____ to   (b) _____ , then to (c)_____ , and finally to   (d)_____ .

5. You begin your trip at a city located at 55°N, 37°E. You leave this city and fly to a city located at 49°N, 123°W. Then you board a plane and fly southeast to a city at 38°N, 77°W, where many famous monuments are located. After spending some time seeing the sights, you fly southeast to a city located at 35°S, 149°E. You traveled from the city of   (a)_____ to   (b) _____ , then to (c)_____ , and finally to   (d)_____ .

Name _____ Date _____

6. Identify the cities located between 15°E and 15°W. Write the cities on the blanks below.

_____

_____

7. Identify the cities located north of 60°N. Write the cities on the blank below.

_____

8. Identify the cities located between 105°E and 180°. Write the names of the cities on the

blanks below.

_____

_____

9. Identify the cities located north of the equator and west of the Prime Meridian. Write the

cities on the blanks below.

_____

_____

_____

10. Identify the cities located south of the equator and east of the Prime Meridian. Write the

cities on the blanks below.

_____

_____

Name_____ Date _____

Latitude and Longitude Practice Exercise 2

Refer to a copy of Map II and complete the following activity.

      Each of the following latitude and longitude coordinates locates a major world city. On the blanks, write the name of the city, continent, and hemispheres where the city is located.

Latitude	Longitude	City	Continent	Hemispheres
1. 41°N	87°W	_____	_____	_____
2. 55°N	37°E	_____	_____	_____
3. 16°N	73°E	_____	_____	_____
4. 14°N	121°E	_____	_____	_____
5. 61°N	149°W	_____	_____	_____
6. 34°S	58°W	_____	_____	_____
7. 34°S	18°E	_____	_____	_____
8. 51°N	0°	_____	_____	_____
9. 30°N	31°E	_____	_____	_____
10. 40°N	2°W	_____	_____	_____
11. 36°N	4°E	_____	_____	_____
12. 31°N	121°E	_____	_____	_____
13. 45°N	75°W	_____	_____	_____
14. 15°N	17°W	_____	_____	_____
15. 35°S	149°E	_____	_____	_____

Name _____ Date _____

Using the Sun to Determine Latitude

     The Sun and other celestial bodies can be used to determine latitude. First, it is important to understand certain facts about the path the Sun's rays travel on the surface of the earth.

     The direct rays of the noonday Sun are always shining overhead at an angle of 90° at some latitude between $23\frac{1}{2}$°N latitude and $23\frac{1}{2}$°S latitude. The name given to the line of latitude at $23\frac{1}{2}$°N is the **Tropic of Cancer**. The name given to the line of latitude at $23\frac{1}{2}$°S is the **Tropic of Capricorn**.

     The direct rays of the Sun shine directly overhead at noon **each day** somewhere between $23\frac{1}{2}$°N and $23\frac{1}{2}$°S. The direct rays of the Sun **never** shine directly overhead at any latitude greater than $23\frac{1}{2}$°N and $23\frac{1}{2}$°S. (See Diagram 9 on page 56.)

Refer to a globe or world map and answer the following questions.

1. The equator represents _____° latitude.

2. Locate $23\frac{1}{2}$°S latitude. This line of latitude is called the

    (Tropic of Cancer/Tropic of Capricorn).

3. Locate $23\frac{1}{2}$°N latitude. This line of latitude is called the

    (Tropic of Cancer/Tropic of Capricorn).

Refer to Diagram 9 and complete the following activity. Circle the correct answers.

4. On December 21 at noon, the direct rays from the Sun are directly overhead at

    (0°, $23\frac{1}{2}$°N, $23\frac{1}{2}$°S).

    This line of latitude is called the (equator/Tropic of Cancer/Tropic of Capricorn).

5. On March 21 at noon, the direct rays from the Sun are directly overhead at

    (0°, $23\frac{1}{2}$°N, $23\frac{1}{2}$°S).

    This line of latitude is called the (equator/Tropic of Cancer/Tropic of Capricorn).

6. On June 21 at noon, the direct rays from the Sun are directly overhead at

    (0°, $23\frac{1}{2}$°N, $23\frac{1}{2}$°S).

    This line of latitude is called the (equator/Tropic of Cancer/Tropic of Capricorn).

    The Sun is shining directly overhead in the (Northern/Southern) Hemisphere.

7. On September 21 at noon, the direct rays from the Sun are directly overhead at

    (0°, $23\frac{1}{2}$°N, $23\frac{1}{2}$°S).

    This line of latitude is called the (equator/Tropic of Cancer/Tropic of Capricorn).

Name _____ Date _____

8. T/F   The direct rays from the Sun are always overhead at noon somewhere between 23 $\frac{1}{2}$°N and 23 $\frac{1}{2}$°S latitude.

9. The direct rays of the Sun shine directly overhead two times per year at the (equator/Tropic of Cancer/Tropic of Capricorn).

   The two dates are (circle two): (December 21/March 21/June 21/September 21).

Diagram 9

Dec. 21   Mar. 21/Sept. 21   June 21

A	B	C	D	E
23 $\frac{1}{2}$°S		0°		23 $\frac{1}{2}$°N

Refer to Diagram 9 above and complete the following.

10. Draw a vertical line from the date on Diagram 9 to the letter representing the latitude where the direct rays of the Sun will be shining at noon on March 21 and September 21.

11. Draw a vertical line from the the date on Diagram 9 to the letter representing the latitude where the direct rays of the Sun will be shining at noon on June 21.

12. Draw a vertical line from the date on Diagram 9 to the letter representing the latitude where the direct rays of the Sun will be shining at noon on December 21.

13. On a date between December 21 and March 21, the direct rays from the Sun will shine directly overhead at the point represented by the letter_____.

14. On a date between March 21 and June 21, the direct rays from the Sun will shine directly overhead at the point represented by the letter_____.

15. On a date between June 21 and September 21, the direct rays from the Sun will shine directly overhead at the point represented by the letter_____.

16. On a date between September 21 and December 21, the direct rays from the Sun will shine directly overhead at the point represented by the letter _____.

Name _____ Date _____

How to Determine Latitude
From the Position of the Sun

Look at Diagram 9 on page 56. Imagine that people are standing where each of the letters is located. Let us assume that it is noon at "D," and the direct rays of the Sun are overhead at "D." The angle of the Sun's rays with the earth's surface at noon at "D" is 90°. The angle of the Sun's rays at noon on this date are indirect or shining at an angle less than 90° at "A," "B," "C," and "E." Knowing that the Sun is directly overhead at "D," the observers at the other locations can determine their latitude.

Using the Sun to determine latitude requires that a number of things be known.

1. The latitude where the direct rays of the Sun will be 90° at noon on a given date must be known. This is the location where the direct rays from the Sun are shining.

2. The angle of the Sun's indirect rays at noon at the same date at a given location must be known. This angle will be less than 90° because the Sun is not directly overhead.

Refer to Diagram 9 to answer the following. Remember, the Sun is directly overhead at "D."

1. The point where the angle of the sun is 90° at noon is _____.

2. The points where the angle of the Sun is less than 90° at noon are _____.

3. The point(s) where the Sun would be seen at an angle less than 90° at noon and to the

   north is/are _____ .

4. The point(s) where the Sun would be seen at an angle less than 90° at noon and to the

   south is/are_____ .

5. True/False   The people at "A" would see the Sun at noon at a lower angle than

   would the people at "B," "C," "D," and "E."

6. True/False   The people at "C" and "E" would see the Sun at the same angle at noon.

7. True/False   The people at "E" would see the Sun at an angle less than 90° and to

   the south.

8. True/False   The people at "C" would see the Sun at an angle less than 90° and to

   the north.

Name _____ Date _____

Refer to Diagram 10 below to complete the following activity.

In Diagram 10, assume the date is March 21. At noon on this date, the direct rays of the Sun will be directly overhead at the equator (0°). Individuals are standing at latitudes "A" (23 ½°S), "B" (0°), and "C" (23 ½°N). Each of the individuals measures the angle the Sun makes with the horizon at noon.

Diagram 10

* Diagram is for illus-
tration purposes only.
The angles are not
drawn precisely.

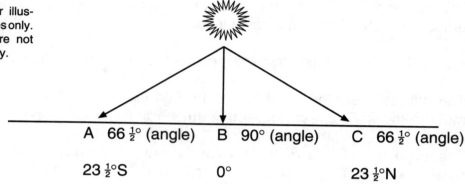

A 66 ½° (angle)   B 90° (angle)   C 66 ½° (angle)

23 ½°S   0°   23 ½°N

9. The individual at "B" sees the Sun _____ overhead at noon.

10. The angle at which "B" sees the Sun at noon is   (a) 23 ½°   (b) 90°   (c) 66 ½°.

11. The angle at which "A" sees the Sun at noon is   (a) 23 ½°   (b) 90°   (c) 66 ½°.

12. The angle at which "C" sees the Sun at noon is   (a) 23 ½°   (b) 90°   (c) 66 ½°.

How do you determine the latitude of each individual? You determine the angle the Sun is shining at the individual's location and subtract it from the angle of the Sun at the location where the noonday Sun is directly overhead. The angle of the Sun at the point where it is directly overhead at noon is 90°.

Example: Individuals at "B" see the Sun directly overhead at noon. The angle of the Sun's rays is 90°. Individuals at "A" see the noonday Sun at an angle of 66 ½° above the horizon to the north.

$$90° - 66 ½° = 23 ½°$$

The latitude of individuals at "A" is 23 ½° south of the point where the Sun is directly overhead. Since the date is March 21, the Sun is directly overhead at the equator (0° latitude). The individuals at "A" are 23 ½° south of 0° latitude; therefore, the latitude of the individuals at "A" is 23 ½°S.

23 ½°S   0°

23 ½°

Name _____ Date _____

13. Individuals at "A" see the Sun at an angle of 66 ½° to the north. Individuals at "A" are

_____ ° south of "B."

14. Individuals at "C" see the Sun at an angle of 66 ½° to the south. Individuals at "C" are

_____ ° north of "B."

At noon on June 21, the direct rays of the Sun are on the Tropic of Cancer. Diagram 11 below shows the Sun directly overhead at noon on the Tropic of Cancer.

Diagram 11

* Diagram is for illustration purposes only. The angles are not drawn precisely.

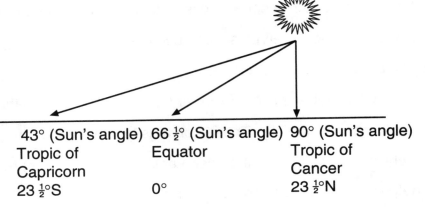

43° (Sun's angle)   66 ½° (Sun's angle)   90° (Sun's angle)
Tropic of   Equator   Tropic of
Capricorn   Cancer
23 ½°S   0°   23 ½°N

An observer at the equator would see the noonday Sun at an angle of 66 ½° above the horizon and to the north. In this case, the noonday Sun's angle is 90° at the Tropic of Cancer. Subtract 90° - 66 ½° = 23 ½°. The observer at the equator is 23 ½° south from the latitude where the Sun's angle is 90° above the horizon. 23 ½° south from 23 ½°N is 0°. The observer's latitude is 0° on the equator.

0°   23 ½°N
└──────────────────────┘
        23 ½°

An observer at the Tropic of Capricorn (23 ½°S) would see the noonday Sun at an angle of 43° above the horizon and to the north. The observer is 47° south of where the Sun is directly overhead at the Tropic of Cancer, which is 23 ½°N latitude. 90° - 43° = 47°. 47° south from 23 ½°N is 23 ½°S. The latitude of the observer is 23 ½°S.

23 ½°S   0°   23 ½°N
└────────────────────────────┘
            47°

Name _____ Date _____

Finding the Latitude From the Angle of the Sun

Read each of the following problems. Determine the latitude location for the observer. Refer to Diagrams 9–11 if necessary.

1. The date is March 21. An observer looks south and sees the noonday Sun at an angle of $66\frac{1}{2}°$ high in the sky. The observer is located in the (a)_____ Hemisphere. The latitude of the observer is (b)_____° (c) N/S.

2. The date is June 21. An observer looks up and sees the noonday Sun at an angle of 90° high in the sky. The observer is located in the (a)_____ Hemisphere. The latitude of the observer is (b)_____° (c) N/S.

3. The date is December 21. An observer looks south and sees the noonday Sun at an angle of 43° high in the sky. The observer is located in the (a) _____ Hemisphere. The latitude of the observer is (b)_____° (c) N/S.

4. The date is December 21. An observer looks south and sees the noonday Sun at an angle of $66\frac{1}{2}°$ high in the sky. The observer is located on the (a) _____. The latitude of the observer is (b)_____°.

5. The date is September 21. An observer looks north and sees the noonday Sun at an angle of $66\frac{1}{2}°$ high in the sky. The observer is located in the (a) _____ Hemisphere. The latitude of the observer is (b)_____° (c) N/S.

6. The date is December 21. An observer looks up and sees the noonday Sun at an angle of 90° high in the sky. The observer is located in the (a)_____ Hemisphere. The latitude of the observer is (b)_____° (c) N/S.

7. The date is June 21. An observer looks north and sees the noonday Sun at an angle of 43° high in the sky. The observer is located in the (a) _____ Hemisphere. The latitude of the observer is (b)_____° (c) N/S.

8. The date is June 21. An observer looks north and sees the noonday Sun at an angle of $66\frac{1}{2}°$ high in the sky. The observer is located on the (a) _____. The latitude of the observer is (b)_____°.

Name _____ Date _____

Sun and Latitude Review

Complete the blanks in #1. Select your answers from the terms below. Some terms may be used more than once.

Tropic of Cancer   **Tropic of Capricorn**   **23½**   **one**

equator   **0**   **two**

1. The direct rays of the Sun are always shining directly overhead at noon somewhere between the (a)_____ of _____ at (b)_____ °N and the (c)_____ of _____ at 23½°S. The direct rays of the Sun shine directly overhead at the (d)_____ at (e)____° two times per year. The first day of summer in the Northern Hemisphere occurs on June 21, when the Sun is directly overhead at the (f)_____ of _____ at 23½°N. The Sun then travels south and crosses the (g) _____ on September 21, which is the first day of autumn in the Northern Hemisphere. The Sun continues on south, and on December 21, the first day of winter in the Northern Hemisphere, the direct rays of the Sun are overhead at the (h)_____ of _____ at 23½°S. The Sun then begins to move back toward the Northern Hemisphere, and on March 21, shines directly overhead at the (i) _____. March 21 is the first day of spring in the Northern Hemisphere. In the period of one year, the Sun will shine directly overhead at the Tropic of Cancer (j)_____ time(s). In the period of one year, the Sun will shine directly overhead at the equator (k)_____ time(s). In the period of one year, the Sun will shine directly overhead at the Tropic of Capricorn (l) _____ time(s).

Complete the blanks in #2. Select your answers from the terms below.

90   **noon**   **overhead**   **angle**

north   **south**   **latitude**

2. To determine latitude using the Sun, you must know the (a)_____where the Sun will be shining directly overhead at (b)_____. You must determine the (c) _____ of the noonday Sun above the horizon at your location. You then subtract the angle at which you see the noonday Sun from (d)_____°. Then subtract the answer from the latitude of the location where the Sun is directly (e)_____. Then you must note if the Sun is (f)_____ or (g) _____ of your location.

61

Name _____ Date _____

Determining Latitude for Locations
Greater Than 23 ½°N and 23 ½°S

The Sun is **never seen directly overhead** on any date throughout the year for those who live at a latitude that is north of 23 ½°N or south of 23 ½°S. In other words, the noonday Sun is never seen at an angle of 90° at these locations. However, one can still determine the latitude for locations in these regions if (1) one knows the latitude where the Sun is directly overhead at noon and (2) one measures the angle of the noonday Sun above the horizon.

Example A: The date is June 21. The observer looks south at noon and sees the Sun at an angle of 40° above the horizon. The observer knows that on June 21, the noonday Sun is directly overhead at an angle of 90° at 23 ½°N latitude.

$$90° - 40° = 50°$$

The observer is 50° from the latitude where the Sun is directly overhead. The latitude where the Sun is directly overhead is 23 ½°N. The observer sees the noonday Sun to the south, so the observer's latitude is 50° north of 23 ½°N.

$$50° + 23\tfrac{1}{2}° = 73\tfrac{1}{2}°$$ The observer's latitude is 73 ½°N.

Example B: The date is June 21. The observer looks north at noon and sees the Sun at an angle of 40° above the horizon. The observer knows that on June 21, the noonday Sun is directly overhead at an angle of 90° at 23 ½°N latitude.

$$90° - 40° = 50°$$

The observer is 50° from the latitude where the Sun is directly overhead. The latitude where the Sun is directly overhead is 23 ½°N. The observer sees the noonday Sun to the north, so the observer's latitude is 50° south of 23 ½°N. In this example, the observer is 50° from the latitude where the Sun is directly overhead, but because it is south, it is necessary to remember that the observer must subtract.

$$50° - 23\tfrac{1}{2}° = 26\tfrac{1}{2}°$$ The observer's latitude is 26 ½°S.

Note that the distance of the observer from the point where the Sun is directly overhead in both examples is 50°. In Example B, moving 50° south of 23 ½°N means crossing the equator and continuing 26 ½° south of the equator. 23 ½° + 26 ½° = 50° (the distance from the latitude where the Sun is directly overhead).

Name _____ Date _____

Answer the following questions. Use the blank space provided to do the math computation.

1. The date is March 21. Observer "B" sees the noonday Sun at an angle of 30° to the south. Observer "B's" latitude is _____° (N/S).

2. The date is September 21. Observer "C" sees the noonday Sun at an angle of 40° to the north. Observer "C's" latitude is _____° (N/S).

3. The date is September 21. Observer "D" sees the noonday Sun at an angle of 20° to the south. Observer "D's" latitude is _____° (N/S).

4. The date is December 21. Observer "E" sees the noonday Sun at an angle of 20° to the south. Observer "E's" latitude is _____° (N/S).

5. The date is June 21. Observer "F" sees the noonday Sun at an angle of 10° to the north. Observer "F's" latitude is _____° (N/S).

Diagram 12

March 21

* Diagram is for illustration purposes only. The angles are not drawn precisely.

Indirect Rays   Indirect Rays

Direct Rays

Angle	50°	70°	90°	70°	50°
Latitude	40°S	20°S	0°	20°N	40°N
Observer	A	B	C	D	E

Example: In Diagram 12, Observer "A" sees the Sun at an angle of 50° to the north. Observer "A" knows the angle of the Sun for Observer "C" is 90°. Observer "C's" latitude is 0°. Observer "A" subtracts 90° - 50° = 40°. Observer "A" knows he or she is 40° south of 0° latitude. 0° - 40° = -40°. The latitude of Observer "A" is 40°S.

Complete the following questions.

6. The Sun is shining directly overhead at Point (a)_____ at an angle of (b) _____°. This point represents (c)_____° latitude.

7. The Points A, B, D, and E on March 21 are receiving (a) (indirect/direct) rays at noon. The angles of these rays are (b) (more/less) than 90°.

8. On March 21, Observer "B" sees the noonday Sun at an angle of 70° to the north. The distance in degrees Observer "B" is from the latitude where the Sun is directly overhead is determined by subtracting: (a) _____° - _____°. Observer "B" is (b)_____° from where the Sun is shining directly overhead. Since it is March 21, the Sun is shining directly overhead at (c) _____°. The latitude of Observer "B" is (d)_____° (e) N/S.

9. Observer "D" is located at _____° latitude (N/S).

10. Observer "E" is located at _____° latitude (N/S).

Name _____ Date _____

Using the Night Sky to Determine Latitude

   Polaris, the North Star, has been used for centuries by ship captains in the Northern Hemisphere to determine their latitudes on clear nights. Polaris can be used to determine latitude because Polaris is directly overhead at the North Pole. Diagram 13 shows the North Star over the North Pole.

   To find Polaris, the North Star, one must find the Big Dipper. The Big Dipper is the name given to a group of stars in the northern sky that appears in the shape of a dipper with a handle. Two stars in the dipper point to the North Star. Diagram 14 shows the stars forming the Big Dipper. The two stars in the dipper are pointing toward the North Star.

Diagram 13

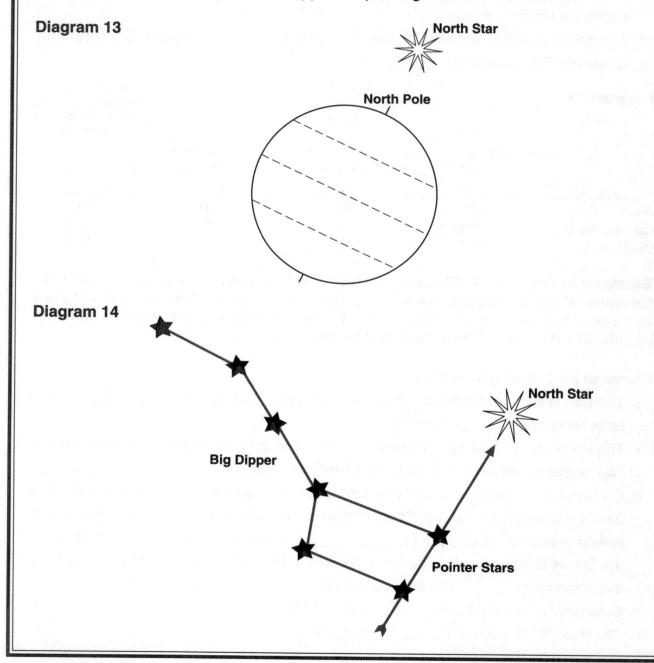

Diagram 14

Name _____ Date _____

    When determining latitude using the North Star, the observer is determining the angle the North Star makes with the horizon. The angle the North Star makes with the horizon at the observer's location determines the observer's latitude.

Diagram 15

To complete the following activity (using Diagram 15), you will need a protractor, ruler, and pencil.

1. Draw a straight line from "A" to "B."
2. Draw a straight line from "B" to "C."
3. Draw a straight line from "B" to "D."
4. Draw a straight line from "B" to "E."
5. Place your protractor on line "B—C" with the center on Point "B."

6. Read the number on the protractor at Point "D". _____ °

The number you read should be 10°. Point "D" makes an angle of 10° with line "B—C," which represents the horizon. This means Observer "D" is located at 10°N latitude. If you did not get this number, check with your teacher before continuing to #7.

7. What angle does Point "E" make with line "B—C"? _____ °

8. What angle does Point "A" make with line "B—C"? _____ °

Assume an observer in the Northern Hemisphere sees the North Star at Points "D," "E," and "A" on different nights. The observer measures the angle the North Star makes with the horizon each night. Write the observer's latitude for each of the following questions.

9. The latitude when the North Star is seen at Point "D" is (a)_____°N. This means that

    the observer is (b)_____ ° from the equator in the (c)_____ Hemisphere.

10. The latitude when the North Star is seen at Point "E" is (a)_____ °N. This means that

    the observer is (b)_____ ° from the equator in the (c)_____ Hemisphere.

11. The latitude when the North Star is seen at Point "A" is (a)_____ °N. This means that

    the observer is (b)_____ ° from the equator in the (c)_____ Hemisphere.

Name _____ Date _____

Finding Latitudes and the Angle of the North Star for Major Cities

You have learned that to determine latitude using Polaris (the North Star) you must determine the angle between the horizon and Polaris. The **angle** between the horizon and the height of the North Star above the horizon will be the latitude for a given location.

Example: An individual is located in the city of Minneapolis, Minnesota. The latitude of the city is listed as 45°N. That evening the individual looks to the night sky and finds the North Star (Polaris). The angle between the horizon and the North Star is 45°. The angle of the North Star is exactly the same as the latitude listed for the city. The individual determined that if the latitude of a specific place is known, then the angle of the North Star is the same as the latitude at that specific place.

Complete the following activity. Use an atlas or a copy of Map II to determine the latitude for each city. This will allow you to determine the angle the North Star will make with the horizon for each city.

City	Latitude	Angle of North Star
1. Chicago, Illinois	____ °N	____ °
2. Paris, France	____ °N	____ °
3. London, England	____ °N	____ °
4. Dakar, Senegal	____ °N	____ °
5. Shanghai, China	____ °N	____ °
6. Anchorage, Alaska	____ °N	____ °
7. Manila, Philippines	____ °N	____ °

Name _____ Date _____

North Star and Latitude Review

Use the terms below to complete the blanks in the following selection. Some terms may be used more than once.

night	**Northern**	**North Star**	**0**	**latitude**
north	**90**	**latitude**	**angle**	

Latitude is the distance in degrees (1) _____ or south from the equator. The latitude at the equator is (2)___°. Polaris, or the (3)_____ _____, can be used to determine latitude in the (4)_____ Hemisphere. To use Polaris to find latitude, the (5)_____ of Polaris above the horizon in the (6)_____ sky must be determined. The angle that Polaris makes with the horizon determines the (7)_____ of the observer. For example, an observer who sees Polaris directly overhead is at (8) _____°N.

9. An **astrolabe** is an instrument that can be used to determine latitude by finding the angle the North Star makes with the horizon. Use an encyclopedia or other source and explain how an astrolabe is used.

_____

_____

_____

_____

_____

_____

_____

_____

_____

_____

_____

Name _____ Date _____

Longitude and Time

It has been agreed by most nations that 0° longitude, or the Prime Meridian, is the point from which time is measured. Longitude can be determined if the time at the Prime Meridian is known and the time at a specific location on earth is known. The earth rotates on its axis 15° each hour. Knowing the time at the Prime Meridian, the time at another specific location on the surface of the earth, and the fact that every hour difference is 15° makes it possible to determine longitude using time.

Example: It is known that the time at the Prime Meridian is 10:00 a.m. The time at Point "A" is 8:00 a.m. The earth rotates 15° per hour. Since there is a difference of two hours between the two locations, we can determine that there is 30° difference in longitude. Since the earth rotates on its axis from west to east, Point "A" is west of the Prime Meridian. This means that places east of Point "A" have already experienced the hour that is occurring at that location.

Diagram 16

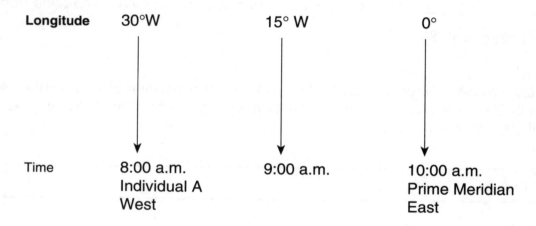

The following charts will help explain how time changes at different longitude locations.

1. The earth rotates on its axis 15° per hour.

2. Time approaches from the east. This means that those places located east of a given location are experiencing a later hour.

Chart I:

Longitude	60°W	45°W	30°W	15°W	0°	15°E	30°E	45°E	60°E
Time	8:00 a.m.	9:00 a.m.	10:00 a.m.	11:00 a.m.	12:00 p.m.	1:00 p.m.	2:00 p.m.	3:00 p.m.	4:00 p.m.

Name _____ Date _____

Chart II: One Hour Later

Longitude	60°W	45°W	30°W	15°W	0°	15°E	30°E	45°E	60°E
Time	9:00 a.m.	10:00 a.m.	11:00 a.m.	12:00 p.m.	1:00 p.m.	2:00 p.m.	3:00 p.m.	4:00 p.m.	5:00 p.m.

Chart III: Two Hours Later

Longitude	60°W	45°W	30°W	15°W	0°	15°E	30°E	45°E	60°E
Time	10:00 a.m.	11:00 a.m.	12:00 p.m.	1:00 p.m.	2:00 p.m.	3:00 p.m.	4:00 p.m.	5:00 p.m.	6:00 p.m.

Complete the following:

1. You are located at 30°E longitude. You check your watch and note the time is exactly 10:00 a.m., Wednesday. The time at the Prime Meridian is ____:00 a.m., Wednesday.

2. You are located at 30°W longitude. You check your watch and note the time is exactly 1:00 p.m., Thursday. The time at the Prime Meridian is ____:00 p.m., Thursday.

3. The time at the Prime Meridian is 12:00 noon. The time at your longitude is 9:00 a.m.

    Your longitude is (circle one):

    (a)   east/west   of the Prime Meridian.

    Your longitude is (circle one):

    (b)   45°E/45°W.

4. Refer to a copy of Map II and Charts I, II, and III. The time at the Prime Meridian is 12:00 noon. (Indicate the time and circle whether it's a.m. or p.m.)

    The time at Chicago (90°W) is   (a) _____ a.m. / p.m.

    The time at Dakar (15°W) is   (b) _____ a.m. / p.m.

    The time at Bombay (75°E) is   (c) _____ a.m. / p.m.

    The time at Manila (120°E) is   (d) _____ a.m. / p.m.

Name _____ Date _____

Can You Find the Survivors?

Use what you have learned about map reading, latitude, longitude, and time to find the locations for the following missing people. Refer to an atlas or world map to locate the survivors.

1. The first message received from a distressed ship indicates the ship is located in the area bounded by 30°N, 20°S, 120°W, 130°W. Trace a line over the boundaries for this region with your finger.

2. Later, a second message is received from the ship captain indicating that the noonday Sun is directly overhead. The date is June 21. The time at the location is 4:00 a.m. The time at the Prime Meridian is noon.

   The location of the ship is exactly _____ °N, _____ °W.

3. A plane crash occurs. Later, a message is received from the survivors indicating that at their location the North Star is seen 60° above the horizon. The message indicates that their time is 2:00 a.m., Thursday, with the time at the Prime Meridian 6:00 p.m., Wednesday.

   The location of the plane survivors is (a)_____ ° _____ , _____ ° _____ in the country (b) _____ .

4. The bus a tourist group is riding experiences mechanical problems. It is necessary to radio for assistance. The driver radios the location of the bus as 30°S, 140°E. The tourist bus is located in the state of (a) _____ in the country of (b) _____ in the (c) _____ and _____ Hemispheres.

Name _____ Date _____

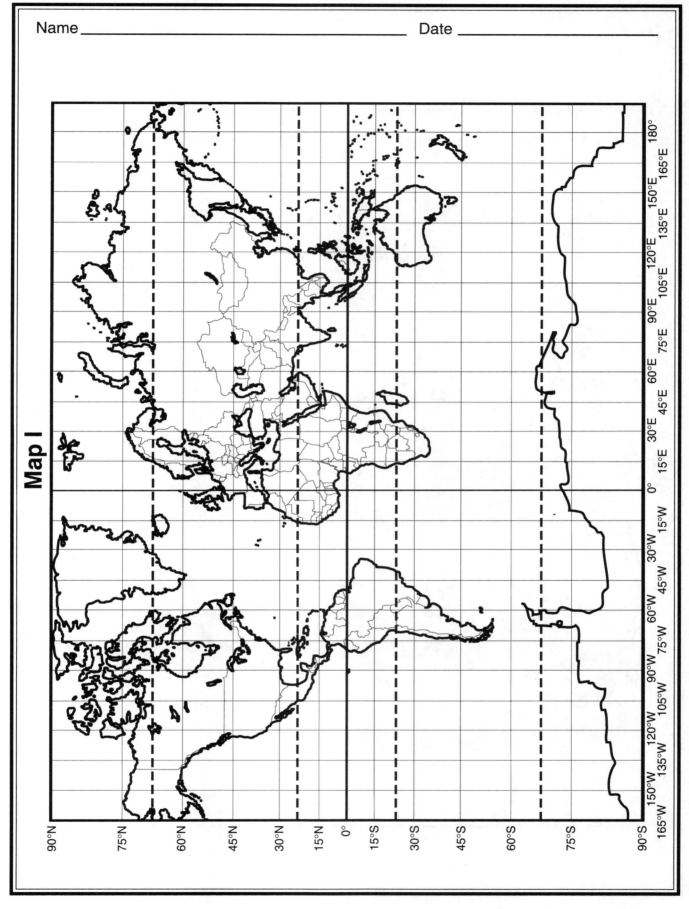

Map I

Name _____ Date _____

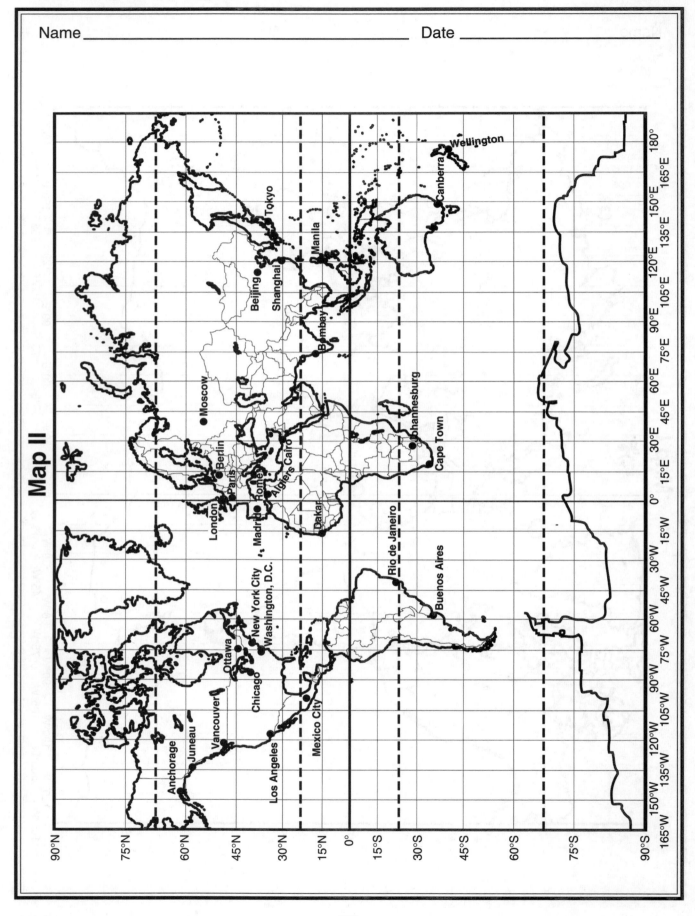

Map II

Answer Keys

Developing Map-Reading Skills (pages 1–2)
1. physical; features on the earth's surface.
2. population; the population density of the area.
3. political; the political boundaries of the area.

1. information
2. physical
3. population
4. climatic
5. compass rose
6. north
7. south

8.   North
    West   East
       South

The Map Legend (page 3)
1. 100   2. 250   3. 500
4. 200   5. 500   6. 1,000
7. 6   8. 15   9. 30

Converting Kilometers to Miles (page 4)
1. 100; 62   2. 250; 155   3. 500; 311
4. 200; 124   5. 500; 311   6. 1,000; 621
7. 6; 3.7   8. 15; 9.3   9. 30; 18.6

Converting Miles to Kilometers (page 5)
1. 200; 320   2. 500; 800   3. 1,000; 1,600
4. 50; 80   5. 125; 200   6. 250; 400
7. 14; 22   8. 35; 56   9. 70; 112

Using a Map Legend (page 6)
1–6. Teacher check symbols.
7a. Mark should be made one inch from starting mark
  b. Mark should be made two inches from starting mark
  c. Mark should be made four inches from starting mark
  d. Mark should be made four and one-half inches from starting mark
  e. Mark should be made five inches from starting mark

Learning More About Map Scale (page 7)
1. 1/50   2. 1/500   3. 1/1,000
4. 1/25   5. 1/5
6. One inch equals ten miles.
7. One inch equals five hundred miles.
8. One inch equals five miles.
9. One inch equals eighty miles.
10. One inch equals one and one-half miles.

State Map Exercise (page 8)
Teacher check.

Comparing Globes and Maps (pages 9–10)
1. 15°W, 15°E
2. 60°N, 75°N
3. 15°W, 15°E
4. 0°, 15°N
5. Teacher check.
6. larger than

7. the same size as
8. True
9. False; The lines of longitude on Diagram 1 meet at the North and South Poles.
10. Since the lines of longitude are parallel and they do not meet at the poles on Diagram 2, the lines on Diagram 2 distort the size of the area of Region A.
11. The distance between the lines of longitude at the location of Region B are the same on Diagram A and Diagram B.

Flat Maps and Round Globes (page 11)
1. larger
2. larger
3. smaller than
4. the same size as
6. do not meet
7. meet
8. All statements are true and are possible explanations.

Dividing a Rectangle Into Quadrants (page 14)
Teacher check.

Developing a Rectangular Coordinate System (pages 15–16)
1–2. Teacher check.
4. b
6. a
7. 60, 120
10. d
12. a
13. 60, 40
14–20. Teacher check.

Learning About Latitude and Longitude: Facts About Latitude (pages 17–18)
1–4. Teacher check.
5. 1   6. 1   7. 1
8. They never cross./They are the same distance apart.
9. parallel, cross
10. $5\frac{1}{2}$ 11. $\frac{1}{4}$ 12. $\frac{1}{4}$ 13. $\frac{1}{4}$
14. True
15. They are always the same distance apart. They never cross.

Great Circles and Latitude (page 19)
1. parallel   2. North, South   3. the equator
4. 0   5. Great

6. Great Circle   7. a   8. 90   9. 90
10. parallel, north, south

Facts About Longitude (pages 20–22)
1–4. Teacher check.
5. 20   6. 20   7. 20
8. line c—d   9. lines a—b and e—f
10. the same   11. c—d   12. a—b, e—f
13. The lines of longitude come closer together near the poles. The lines of longitude are not parallel.
14. 35   15. 69
16. 20; 700   17. 20; 1,380   18. 20; 700

Great Circles and Longitude (page 23)
1. True   2. east, west   3. a
4. a   5. 180   6. 180
7. meet

How Latitude and Longitude Help to Locate Places on Earth (pages 24–26)
2. North Atlantic Ocean, South Atlantic Ocean
3. Africa, Europe (Iceland), Antarctica
4. Iceland, Senegal, Gambia, Western Sahara, Mauritania
5. Northern, Southern, Western
7. North Atlantic Ocean, Arabian Sea, Pacific Ocean
8. North America, Asia, Africa
9. Honduras, India, Chad, The Philippines, Vietnam, Senegal
10. Northern, Eastern, Western
12. Baltic Sea, Arctic Ocean, Mediterranean Sea
13. Europe, Africa, Antarctica
14. Italy, Sweden, Libya, Chad, Angola
15. Northern, Southern, Eastern
17. Indian Ocean, Pacific Ocean, South Atlantic Ocean
18. South America, Australia, Africa
19. Mozambique, Australia, Angola, Peru, Brazil, Bolivia
20. Southern, Eastern, Western
21. Russia, Iran, Arctic Ocean, Kara Sea, Arabian Sea, Indian Ocean, Kazakstan, Uzbekistan, Turkmenistan, Antarctica
22. Arctic Ocean, Greenland, Canada, North Atlantic Ocean, Venezuela, Guyana, Brazil, Bolivia, Paraguay, Argentina, Falkland Islands, Antarctica, South Atlantic Ocean

Measuring Degrees of Longitude (page 27)
Teacher check student work on diagram.
4. c   8. c   9. a   11. a

Reviewing Latitude and Longitude 1 (pages 29–30)
1. a   2. b   3. Prime Meridian   4. equator
6. North, South   7. east, west
8. d   9. d   10. c
12. b   14. a   16. d

Identifying Hemispheres (pages 31–32)
1. a   2. c   3. d   4. b   5. c
6. a   7. b   8. a   9. c   10. d

Locating Lines of Latitude and Longitude (page 33)
1–2. Teacher check.
3. 180   4. yes   5. yes   6. yes   7. yes
8. c   9. c   10. 30   11. 30   12. north
13. Argentina, Brazil, Paraguay, Bolivia
14. Saudi Arabia, Egypt, Israel

Using Latitude and Longitude to Locate Areas on a Map (page 34)
1. 120, 150   2. 0, 30
3. 60, 90   4. 0, 30
5–10. Teacher check map work.

Latitude and Longitude Crossword Puzzle (page 35)

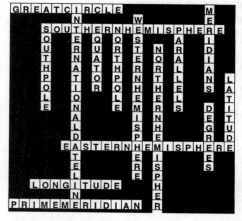

Reviewing Longitude and Latitude 2 (pages 36–37)
1. 0, North   2. Prime   3. England
4. International Date Line   5. 180
6. b   7. c   8. a   9. a   10. b
11. b   12. a   13. a
14. b, c, and d should be marked with a plus
15. a, c, and d should be marked with a plus
16. Longitude: b, e, g, h, j
    Latitude: a, c, d, f, i

Where on Earth is This Location? (page 38)
Teacher check map work.

Where is This City Located? (page 38)
1. F   2. M   3. A   4. E   5. J
6. H   7. C   8. N   9. D   10. O
11. I   12. G   13. B   14. K   15. L

Converting Degrees of Latitude and Longitude to Miles and Kilometers (pages 39–40)
1. 160   2. 240   3. 320   4. 800   5. 1,600
6a. 15; b. 1,035; c. 1,656
7a. 90; b. 6,210; c. 9,936
8a. 75; b. 5,175; c. 8,280
9a. 150; b. 10,350; c. 16,560
10a. 40; b. 2,760; c. 4,416
11a. 180; b. 12,420; c. 19,872; e. !s

Distance in Degrees and Miles/Kilometers at Various Latitudes (pages 41–42)
1a. 10°N; b. 20°N; c. 30°N; d. 40°N; e. 50°N; f. 60°N; g. 70°N
2. T
3. F; The diameter of each circle is different.
4. F; The circumference of each circle is different.
5a. 24,840; b. 39,744
6a. 21,600; b. 34,560
7a. 12,600; b. 20,160

74

Measuring Longitude and Latitude in Miles and Kilometers (pages 43–45)
Chart I:

	Latitude	Longitude	Miles from Equator	Miles from Prime Meridian
1.	0°	78°W	0	5,382
2.	30°N	31°E	2,070	1,860
3.	60°N	11°E	4,140	385
4.	58°N	135°W	4,002	4,725
5.	1°N	103°E	69	7,107
6.	31°N	121°E	2,139	7,260
7.	30°N	90°W	2,070	5,400
8.	31°N	82°W	2,139	4,920

Chart II:

	Kilometers from Equator	Kilometers from Prime Meridian
1.	0	8,611
2.	3,312	2,976
3.	6,624	616
4.	6,403	7,560
5.	110	11,371
6.	3,422	11,616
7.	3,312	8,640
8.	3,422	7,872

1. 3,600; 5,760   2. 2,070; 3,312
3. 5,175; 8,280   4. 8,100; 12,960
5. 2,070; 3,312

Latitude True/False (page 46)
1. T
2. F; All line of latitude are circles of 360°.
3. F; The distance around the earth is different at different latitudes.
4. F; A degree of longitude at 30°N latitude and 70°N latitude represents different numbers of miles.
5. T
6. T
7. F; The distance around the earth in miles is less at 60°N than at 30°N.
8. T
9. T
10. F; Latitude extends from 0° to 90°N and from 0° to 90°S.
11. T

Longitude True/False (page 47)
1. T
2. T
3. F; The equator is not a line of longitude./The equator is a line of latitude.
4. F; Each line of longitude is not parallel to another line of longitude.
5. F; All lines of longitude meet at the North Pole and the South Pole.
6. F; Longitude measures distance east and west from the Prime Meridian.
7. F. The distance (in kilometers) between 10°E and 10°W at 10°N latitude is different than at 60°N latitude.
8. T
9. F; The International Date Line represents 180° longitude.
10. T
11. T

Review Exercise (pages 48–49)
Teacher check map work.
2. 2,070   3. 3,312   4. 7,200   5. 11,520
6. 2,070   7. 3,312
14. United States   21. Australia
24. 15°S, 150°W   25. 30°S, 30°W
26. 60°S, 45°W   27. 10°S, 165°W
28. 45°S, 90°W
29. Colombia   30. Brazil

Latitude and Longitude Atlas Activities (pages 50–51)
1. Ireland, Scotland
2. Ireland, Belgium, England, Denmark, Northern Ireland
3. Germany, Austria, Denmark, Northern Ireland, England, Wales, Ireland, Switzerland
4. Spain, Portugal
5. Guatemala, Mexico, United States
6. Haiti, Panama, Nicaragua, Mexico, Dominican Republic, Jamaica, Cuba, United States
7. Canada, Mexico, Guatemala, United States
8. Nigeria, Gambia, Liberia, Ghana, Senegal, Mali, Sierra Leone
9. Mauritania, Morocco
10. Egypt
11. Turkey, Iran, Saudi Arabia, Afghanistan, Pakistan, Iraq, Israel
12. Malaysia, Indonesia

Latitude and Longitude Practice Exercise 1 (pages 52–53)
1a. Rio de Janeiro, b. Canberra, c. Moscow, d. Ottawa
2a. Anchorage, b. Dakar, c. Shanghai
3a. Rio de Janeiro, b. Madrid, c. Paris, d. London
4a. Chicago, b. Dakar, c. Buenos Aires, d. Cape Town
5a. Moscow, b. Vancouver, c. Washington, D.C., d. Canberra
6. Berlin, London, Paris, Rome, Madrid, Algiers
7. Anchorage
8. Canberra, Wellington, Beijing, Manila, Shanghai, Tokyo
9. Dakar, Madrid, Mexico City, Los Angeles, Washington, D.C., New York City, Chicago, Ottawa, Vancouver, Juneau, Anchorage
10. Johannesburg, Cape Town, Canberra, Wellington

Latitude and Longitude Practice Exercise 2 (page 54)

City	Continent	Hemispheres
1. Chicago	North America	N/W
2. Moscow	Europe	N/E
3. Bombay	Asia	N/E
4. Manila	Asia	N/E
5. Anchorage	North America	N/W
6. Buenos Aires	South America	S/W
7. Cape Town	Africa	S/E
8. London	Europe	N/E/W
9. Cairo	Africa	N/E
10. Madrid	Europe	N/W
11. Algiers	Africa	N/E
12. Shanghai	Asia	N/E
13. Ottawa	North America	N/W
14. Dakar	Africa	N/W
15. Canberra	Australia	S/E

Using the Sun to Determine Latitude (pages 55–56)
1. 0   2. Tropic of Capricorn   3. Tropic of Cancer
4. 23½°S, Tropic of Capricorn
5. 0°, equator
6. 23½°N, Tropic of Cancer, Northern
7. 0°, equator
8. T   9. equator, March 21/September 21
10. Line from Mar. 21/Sept. 21 to letter C
11. Line from June 21 to letter E
12. Line from Dec. 21 to letter A
13. B   14. D   15. D   16. B

How to Determine Latitude From the Position of the Sun (pages 57–59)
1. D   2. A, B, C, E   3. A, B, C   4. E
5. True 6. True 7. True 8. True
9. directly   10. b   11. c   12. c
13. 23½°   14. 23½°

Finding the Latitude From the Angle of the Sun (page 60)
1a. Northern, b. 23½, c. N
2a. Northern, b. 23½, c. N
3a. Northern, b. 23½, c. N
4a. equator, b. 0
5a. Southern, b. 23½, c. S
6a. Southern, b. 23½, c. S
7a. Southern, b. 23½, c. S
8a. equator, b. 0

Sun and Latitude Review (page 61)
1a. Tropic of Cancer   b. 23½°
 c. Tropic of Capricorn   d. equator
 e. 0   f. Tropic of Cancer
 g. equator   h. Tropic of Capricorn
 i. equator   j. one
 k. two   l. one

2a. latitude   b. noon
 c. angle   d. 90
 e. overhead   f. north/south
 g. south/north

Determining Latitude for Locations Greater Than 23½°N and 23½°S (pages 62–63)
1. 60, N   2. 50, S   3. 70, N
4. 46½, N   5. 56½, S
6a. C, b. 90, c. 0
7a. indirect, b. less
8a. 90, 70, b. 20, c. 0, d. 20, e. S
9. 20, N   10. 40, N

Using the Night Sky to Determine Latitude (pages 64–65)
1–4. Teacher check student work on diagram.
6. 10   7. 45   8. 90
9a. 10, b. 10, c. Northern
10a. 45, b. 45, c. Northern
11a. 90, b. 90, c. Northern

Finding Latitudes and the Angle of the North Star for Major Cities (page 66)

	Latitude	Angle of North Star
1.	41°N	41°
2.	48°N	48°
3.	51°N	51°
4.	15°N	15°
5.	31°N	31°
6.	62°N	61°
7.	14°N	14°

North Star and Latitude Review (page 67)
1. north   2. 0   3. North Star
4. Northern 5. angle 6. night
7. latitude 8. 90
9. The word *astrolabe* is derived from *astro* "star" and *labio* "finder." An astrolabe was used to measure the altitudes of stars or the Sun to determine latitude and time. By measuring the altitude of the North Star, one can determine one's latitude. By measuring the altitude of the Sun and stars, one can determine the time at one's location.

An astrolabe consists of two flat circular discs. One disc is called the rete. It contains a star map showing the bright stars and the path of the Sun and planets. The other disc is the tympan. It shows the zenith, the horizon, and the lines of altitude and azimuth for a specific latitude. The hours of the day are engraved on the rim of the astrolabe.

On the back of the astrolabe, a circle of degrees is engraved around the edge. One sights along a bar called the alidade to measure the altitude of the Sun or star. Then the rete is turned until the proper star point is over the indicated altitude line on the tympan. One can then read the altitude and azimuth of the stars above the horizon.

Longitude and Time (pages 68–69)
1. 8
2. 3
3a. west, b. 45°W
4a. 6:00 a.m.
 b. 11:00 a.m.
 c. 5:00 p.m.
 d. 8:00 p.m.

Can You Find the Survivors? (page 70)
2. 23½°N, 120°W
3a. 60°N, 120°E; b. Russia
4a. South Australia, b. Australia, c. Southern, Eastern